I0485932

# EMPLOYEE TO EMPLOYER IN 90 DAYS

# MAKE A WAY® MINISTRIES INC

*Employee to Employer In <u>90</u> Days*

Copyright © September 2006 by Rev. William Miller
Updated September, 2015 and June, 2016

MAKE A WAY® PUBLISHING
Miami, Florida

MAKE A WAY® MINISTRIES is a nonprofit Christian Ministry

Operating Office:
P.O. Box 1164
Granbury, Texas 76048

Corporate Office:
12030 SW 129 Court
Suite 104
Miami, Florida 33186

1-800-357-4223

www.makeaway.net
www.creditcounseling.net

**ISBN-10:** 1518622410
**ISBN-13:** 978-1518622410

# Introduction

Many people dream about going into business for themselves instead of working for someone else all their lives. There is an attraction to being more in control of one's own destiny with the possibility of achieving a level of income far surpassing what one could expect in someone else's organization.

The truth is though most of us never quite get past the dreaming stage unless we're forced into it. There's a lot of uncertainty about how to get started and there's uncertainty about what kind of business to get into. Most of us are easily discouraged in the face of so much uncertainty. And we see also that a lot of people fail at it which is scary.

Nevertheless, there are a lot of people who ought to be in business for themselves instead of staying in their comfort places. And in fact, there isn't a lot of security anymore working for other people anyway. So it's something to consider, and this publication can help you get started on your due diligence for making your ultimate decision.

This repost is not an exhaustive study and should be considered with other publications that help to explain how to go into business for oneself. In addition, all users of this book are urged before taking any action to consult with their church leaderships, financial professionals and/or legal counsel to clarify any issues that weren't fully understood.

Also, if you try this and get stuck some place, please don't hesitate to give us a call and we can hopefully get you over a hump just by talking about it. More than anything we want you to succeed by finding your special "blessing place."

# Dedication

This book is dedicated to future entrepreneurs who have the courage to step out boldly to risk their capital and their reputations in the pursuit of a better lifestyle for their families by becoming part of the greatest economic system the world has ever known: free enterprise capitalism based on righteous ethics and morals.

# Content

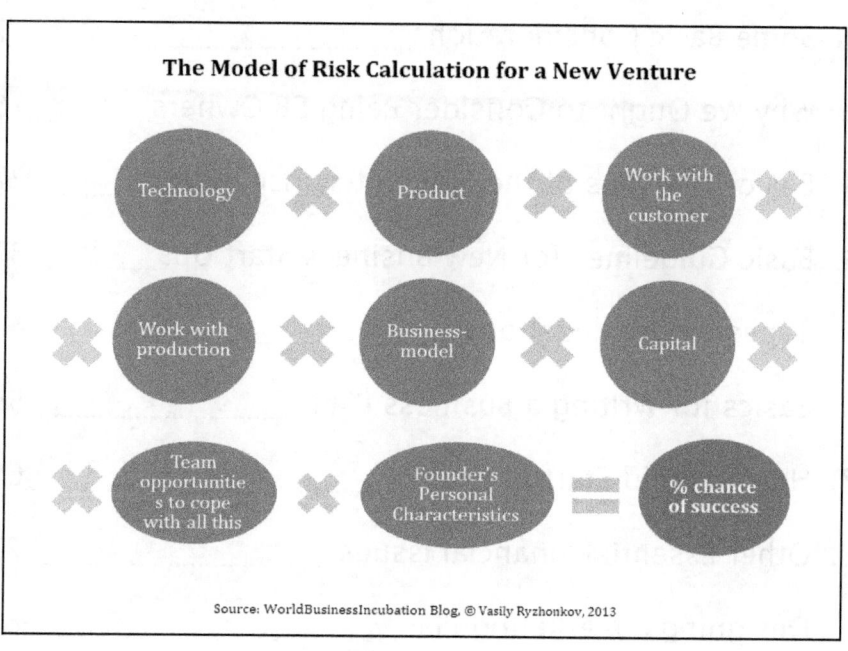

The Model of Risk Calculation for a New Venture

Source: WorldBusinessIncubation Blog, © Vasily Ryzhonkov, 2013

6

# 1. Some Basic Considerations

**M**any people dream all their lives about going into business for themselves Instead of working for others. There's an attraction to being more in control of one's own destiny with the possibility of achieving a level of income that could far surpass what one could expect by working for others. And of course, a business owner can go on vacation whenever he/she wants to and doesn't have to take orders from some *"less than competent supervisor who's only looking out for the company."*

These thoughts do indeed beckon us to take a closer look at the potential paradise of entrepreneurship. In fact almost 1.5 million new businesses were created in the U.S. in 2015 resulting in a total small business population across the country of more than 23 million companies. And, over the next 5 years that's expected to grow by at least an additional 9 million more small businesses.

Just so you see the picture more fully, small business is a big deal in this country:[1]

> 86% of all new jobs
> 75% of all new businesses
> 60% of the existing work force
> 45% of all sales
> 40% of total GNP

---

[1] *"Starting and Running a Profitable Small Business,"* Texas Wesleyan University

The fact is there are so many new small businesses coming on line that the United States is in the midst of a massive cultural shift from a managerial to an entrepreneurial society.[2] Yes, there are some really large corporations out there in the marketplace but only 40% of the workforce is actually employed by them and that number is projected to decline to 30% by the year 2025.

Now from the start you need to know how a SMALL BUSINESS is officially defined. That definition is in the hands of the federal government including the SBA so as you might expect, there's considerable complexity involved. Generally, the determination of the official company size is made according to either its number of employees or the amount of its gross revenue. Moreover, that definition varies by the industry in which the company operates. If a particular company wants to borrow against an SBA guarantee, an official determination must be made as to the "size" of the company to know if it qualifies as a "small" business. Keeping in mind that a lot of variation is involved, we can say that in general the number of employees of a "small" business is less than 100 and/or the annual sales revenue is less than 7.5 million dollars with a lot of exceptions to be expected when you look up the law. Here are a couple of URL addresses to go to as of summer 2016 for further info:

- https://www.sba.gov/sites/default/files/files/Size_Standards_Table.pdf

---

[2] John Naisbitt, *"Megatrends"*

- https://www.sba.gov/contracting/getting-started-contractor/make-sure-you-meet-sba-size-standards/table-small-business-size-standards

Before you get so excited about jumping in with this crowd that you lose your caution, the WISE prospective business owner needs to at least be aware of a few hurdles to be dealt with. It's not about whether you ought to start a small business. You SHOULD start one... *someday!* It's about the timing. You need to assess whether or not you're *ready to make the jump*. As you'll see later, success is all about timing and preparation and knowledge, and I'm pretty sure you want to be successful. With the right training and equipping, almost anybody can be a successful small business owner. But it's not a one-sided, rose-colored opportunity or everybody would already be successful small business millionaires:

- The first thing you need to know is that statistics show that of all the small companies started in the United States in the last 50 years, more than 70 percent of them failed and shut down during their first five years of operation. *Oops!* You absolutely must understand why this happened BEFORE you make the jump.

- When those small businesses were shut down, their owners were often left with responsibility for the debts of their failed companies and had to experience the heartache of personal bankruptcy.

- The proportion of failures to total startups is greater now than it was 50 years ago because the administrative requirements of business management are more complex. Most small business owners start out with almost NO business management knowledge even though without it, the probability of failure is at that very high 70+ percent level. On the other hand if you DO possess the necessary business knowledge, there's at least a 93% chance that you WILL succeed.[3]

- The principal reason small businesses fail in such a high proportion is a combination of under capitalization plus the mismanagement of whatever amount of capital that _was_ available. The main cause is that most new entrepreneurs tend to be sales and operations-oriented instead of fully-administratively-and-financially-prepared MANAGERS of an ongoing serious enterprise.

- Most small business owners don't take a real vacation during the first five years of operation. Whenever they do take time off, they're constantly in contact with their companies or at least thinking about them. They worry about leaving their "baby" with a hired "nanny."

- On average most small businesses produce a level of income for their entrepreneur-owners that's lower than they could make working for someone else which connects to the likelihood that more than 70% will fail.

---

[3] _"Starting and Running a Profitable Small Business,"_ Texas Wesleyan University

Now most of the negatives can be largely overcome with proper planning, preparation and instruction. The biggest need is understanding the area of business finances including budgeting, keeping books, managing bank accounts, understanding how cash flow works, etc. There are many good reasons to consider going into business for yourself, as we'll see in the next chapter, but step into it fully prepared so you will SUCCEED.

Once you're prepared, YOU can succeed if you really want to and if you believe you can do it. First SEE yourself doing something successfully in your "mind's eye" and then go and do it. If you can SEE it, you can DO it. THIS IS A BASIC PRINCIPLE OF BUSINESS. It's not just words!

In addition to seeing it, make it a point to SAY it. Speak out your dreams as if they're in the process of being realized. Speak out your success as if you're already experiencing it. Make what you SAY agree with what you can SEE. What you SEE and SAY determine what you receive and what you become. You are who you SAY you are and stay away from people who're SEEING and SAYING something different either about you or about what you're trying to accomplish.

The truth is, success in business is more a matter of one's attitude and thinking than how hard you work. What you believe about yourself is what you will become! But your eventual SUCCESS will be directly related to the amount of business and financial knowledge you possess when you make the start up. The critical time is the start up. The odds are against you if you start off wrong!

You don't have to learn everything in this book before you start your company, but you DO need to know the basics and you MUST have the right priorities about operating your own company: financial performance will ALWAYS be your first priority! And you MUST understand these things BEFORE you start your company.

If you apply yourself, you can be ready in less than 90 days!

ONE OF THE BEST REASONS I CAN THINK OF
TO BE A SMALL BUSINESS OWNER

# 2. Why We Ought to Be Small Business Owners

Despite a few negatives, there are some really good reasons to consider starting one's own business. For one thing, those that *do* ultimately succeed usually wind up being a lot more financially well off than their counterparts who work for someone else. Statistics show that the income levels of <u>successful</u> entrepreneurs are at least 50% higher on average than comparable folks who're working for others and 50% higher than the salary they had with the company they worked for before they started their own businesses.

The <u>successful</u> ones eventually get to the place where they can take a few days off once in a while. And, there's a great deal of satisfaction derived from watching one's "baby" grow up to become a viable and successful adult.

There's also the fact that once you get rolling along in your own company, you won't have to worry about being down-sized and laid off suddenly without income. In general, the highs of entrepreneurship are higher than the highs of working for somebody else but occasionally the lows are lower. When things are going good, the entrepreneur is euphoric; in times of crisis there's desperation and concern and worry and indecisiveness and lack of sleep. The biggest challenge is to get the business to a point where you can get rid of those lows!

The truth is, owning your own small business can and should be an exciting, challenging and rewarding experience, and there are at least seven important reasons for you to consider starting one, *as soon as you're ready:*

1. The pursuit of <u>Independence</u> is the first reason which includes freedom from having your future in someone else's hands, freedom from endless meetings where little is ever accomplished, freedom from dealing with never-ending boss emergencies instead of your own priorities, freedom from office politics and backbiting and interacting with all those difficult people every day and freedom from having to make money for somebody else's pocket instead of yours. You'll also like the freedom of setting your own schedule so you can work the hours you want to, day or night.

   But most of all, you'll no longer be DEPENDENT upon others and under their control in the pursuit of your personal goals and objectives. You'll be free to allow God to lead you to your destiny without interference from a disinterested employer who requires you to work toward THEIR goals and objectives sometimes in ways that violate your sense of values and direction.

2. The second reason for starting a small business is to enjoy the <u>challenge</u> of having something fun to do where you can be creative and receive the benefits of your creativity. Also, other people will no longer be able to take credit for your ideas.

3. The third reason to start small business is to have a better testimony. For some reason, people who are self-employed are looked up to in our society. It's like a status symbol. Even if you're struggling in your self-employment, you'll be looked up to and admired for trying to make something happen on your own especially if it's known that God is your CEO. The truth is, the people who're working for others that you come in contact with will be ENVIOUS of what you're trying to accomplish. They see you and wish they had the boldness and the courage to try it themselves.

4. The fourth reason is that there are <u>NO external restrictions</u> for the owner of a small business to have to deal with as there often are working for others. External restrictions include the amount of education you have, what gender you are, you age or race or background. Any of these things can hold people back in their careers and RESTRICT their advancement even when their job performance is at the highest level.

5. Another really good reason is that owning a small business can help you <u>build an estate</u> for your family to a much higher level than would be typical working for somebody else. You will be building something substantial for the generations of your progeny to own and benefit from in the future

6. Owning your own business may also allow you to spend more time with your spouse and children, particularly if you provide them with employment. If

you decide to run a home-based small business, you will also be freeing up much of your time and expense that were used in commuting to an employer's office.

7. Finally, every family should consider starting a small business as a way of <u>reducing the amount of tax</u> you pay so you can redirect those funds to expansion of your retirement savings. This is a really important topic that should be emphasized: virtually ALL families in America could and *should* OWN A SMALL BUSINESS FOR THE PURPOSE OF TAX OPTIMIZATION. The U.S. Congress and the U.S. Internal Revenue Service have structured the tax code to favor and encourage the formation of small businesses. So why would we not organize ourselves to get the maximum benefit out of the economic system that's been set up? Why would we persist in paying more taxes than we legally have to by ignoring a principal means that's been created precisely for the purpose of encouraging American entrepreneurship through the incentive of paying lower taxes?

## Special Thoughts for Christian Entrepreneurs

From a Christian perspective, it is our hope that more Believers will aspire to being small business owners because when you're working for someone else, you become dependent on your employer for your well being instead of God. As long as you're employed, your salary payments arrive every week or two automatically and you enjoy certain benefits that are at least partially paid for by your employer. You become involved in a career and the health of your career instead of the health of your spirit. If you're asked to transfer to a new location and you turn it down, your career will suffer. So you will accept job transfers without regarding the possibility that God might want you to stay where you are. You accept job transfers to receive a salary increase without considering that God is your real Provider. It's often difficult for Believers to work for someone else and remain pure in their faith.

By being in business for yourself, you can also work on what God tells you is best for the Kingdom of God and on commercial activities that are consistent with your callings and abilities. You won't be a square peg in a round hole unless you get there by a wrong decision, but if that happens you can just go find a square hole.

In my own life I've been in both places. For the first part of my business career I worked for one of the largest corporations in the world even though I knew my calling was to be in business for myself. I went there to learn about business and intended to leave after five years to apply my new practical business knowledge to my own endeavors. But there was a lot of security in that big corporation including medical insurance, a matching savings plan, an upwardly mobile career track based on good performance, regular salary increases and the assurance of knowing that on a certain day of each month, my bank account would automatically increase.

The five years turned into ten and then got to be twenty before I knew it. Most of the time during those last ten years I was miserable, knowing that I should have been doing something else, resenting that the corporation had control of my life and that I was totally _addicted_ to the financial SECURITY it made available to me.

Eventually, the time came when for personal reasons I had to turn down a transfer to a foreign country and I knew that my future would never recover from not doing what they had wanted me to do. So when the opportunity came to get paid for leaving the company, I accepted early retirement so I could start my own business.

As I write this update in 2016, I have now been involved in my own business for thirty-one years. I've had some ups and I've had some downs. But truthfully I've never regretted finally escaping the "bondage" of the big company to go out and be on my own. Perhaps it wouldn't have been for everybody but it was definitely right for me.

If you're reading this book and you KNOW your destiny is to be self-employed, go on and start preparing yourself for it. Make it your personal goal that you're constantly working toward. Eventually you WILL succeed and then you'll be really glad you took a chance. I believe most people are called to own small business. God has given you wisdom and witty inventions for the purpose of establishing His kingdom. The time will come, perhaps it's now, to step out in faith and pursue your destiny.

# ILLUSTRATION: EFFECT OF SMALL BUSINESS OWNERSHIP ON PERSONAL INCOME TAX

As discussed elsewhere in this publication we recommend that EVERYBODY consider starting a small business for the purpose of tax optimization. It could be a simple side business that's been drawn from the 55 ideas listed at the end of this chapter or it could be any new idea based on your own interests and creativity. Following is a TYPICAL comparison to show the effect on federal tax from owning your own small business:

| | Employee Only | Small Business Owner (DBA) |
|---|---|---|
| **Revenue:** | | |
| Salary from W-2 Employer | $30,000 | 30,000 |
| Income from Own Business | - 0 - | - 0 - |
| (Small Business assumed to break even) | | |
| **Business Deductions:** | | |
| Business Trips (vacation) | - 0 - | 2,000 |
| Children on Payroll | - 0 - | 4,000 |
| Automobile | - 0 - | 4,000 |
| Office in Home | - 0 - | 3,000 |
| Entertainment (one-half) | - 0 - | 2,000 |
| Purchase of Equipment ` | - 0 - | 5,000 |
| Miscellaneous | - 0 - | 2,000 |
| **Adjusted Gross Income:** | $30,000 | 8,000 |
| **Federal Taxes:** | | |
| Income Taxes | 2,800 | - 0 - |
| Social Security | 2,250 | 1,200 |
| Total Taxes Paid | 5,050 | 1,200 |

The illustration on the previous page shows that the tax savings from operating a small business out of this family's home while continuing to work for a W-2 employer was $3,850 via the tax reduction from taking advantage of LEGAL small business deductions to reduce the amount of income that is subject to taxation.[4]

According to IRS Tax Regulations the small business owner is allowed to take business deductions when the following criteria are met:

> The deductions are legal
> The deductions are ordinary for the industry
> The deductions are reasonable
> The deductions are for necessary expenses

Just so you know, there are presently more than 120 legal tax deductions for small businesses embedded somewhere in the 93 thousand pages of the IRS Tax Code. The foregoing example only scratches the surface of what small business people can learn about tax optimization.

In sum, it will be poor stewardship of God's money to not start a small business unless of course He's telling you not to for other reasons. Pray about it, take it to the Lord and if He releases you into small business ownership, you could join the millions of people who're taking this route to make more funds available through the reduction of their taxes.

---

[4] Ibid

# TOP 55 IDEAS FOR SMALL BUSINESS STARTUPS[5]

Following is a list of the most popular small business ideas with an expected startup cost of less than $5,000. Use it to stimulate your thinking for your own company.

**GROUP ONE:**
**$1,500 or less to start up**

Accountant

Boat Cleaning

Bicycle Repair

Business Plan Service

Chimney Sweep

Cleaning Service

Computer Repair

Consultant

Dog Breeder

EBay Assistant

Editorial Services

Electronics Repair

Event Planning

Expert Witness service

Financial Planner

Flea Market

Golf Coach

Home Energy Auditor

Home Inspection

Household Organizer

Import/Export Specialist

Interior Decorator

Jewelry Making

Marketing Copy Writer

Notary

Personal Concierge

Personal Trainer

Property Manager

Small Engine Repair

Solar Energy Consultant

Tax Preparer

Taxidermist

Upholstering

Used Book Sales

---

[5] *https://www.entrepreneur.com/article/201588*

## GROUP TWO:
### $1,500 TO $3,000 to start up

| | |
|---|---|
| Appliance Repair | Herbal Farm Stand |
| Computer Training | Landscaper |
| Desktop Publisher | Massage Therapist |
| Fence Installation | Moving Service |
| Freelance Graphics Designer | Music Lessons |
| Gift Basket Service | Photographer |
| Graffiti Removal | Rug Cleaning |
| Hairstylist | Website Developer |

## GROUP THREE:
### $3,000 TO $5,000 to start up

Bed and Breakfast

Christmas Sales

Day Care

Pet Sitting

Certainly this isn't an exhaustive list but it should get you thinking. Compare this list to things you're passionate about or that occupy your thoughts or that might already involve you in some kind of hobby. Pray about it and ask the Lord what He wants you to do for the Kingdom. But before you start something, be SURE about what you want to do, sure enough to invest adequate time in getting yourself prepared to be a success.[6]

---

[6] Excerpted from: "55 Surefire Home Based Businesses You Can Start for Under $5,000." *By Entrepreneur Press & Cheryl Kimball (2009).*

THE RIGHT TO
PROFIT FREELY
AND BELIEF IN GOD
ARE THE ESSENTIAL
BASES OF FREE ENTERPRISE

# 3. Basic Principles of the Free Enterprise System

Starting a small business will put you smack in the middle of America's free enterprise system. It just happens to be THE economic system that has produced the highest standard of living in the history of the world and you are thinking about how to become a bigger part of it so you can receive more from it like so many millions of people have before you. Some have succeeded and some have failed, but one of the great things about our system is that if you fail, you can get up and try again. And you can keep trying until you finally experience the fulfillment of all your personal dreams and aspirations.

Most people in the world don't have this opportunity because they aren't FREE on a political level. Instead of governing themselves, they have rulers who have taken away their FREEDOM and imposed controls over the details of whatever economic system they have in place. By instituting controls though, the motivation for personal achievement is stifled and people stop trying to succeed financially when the profit incentive has been removed or become so controlled and regulated that only a few can achieve success.

We live in a time when everything is criticized by somebody. The Free Enterprise System is not exempted from the criticism but most of the people doing the criticizing have no clue what they're talking about. They don't actually DO much of anything except take what they can get from other people while living their lives for the most part being uninformed and lacking in wisdom. Instead of doing something constructive to lift themselves out of their failures, they stand by blaming others and criticizing everything they can think of including the best economic system in world history that they've elected not to be a part of. Many of them want to be Socialists and have the government run everything and the reason is that they're too lazy to perform some basic research on the Internet to find out about all the failure Socialism has produced for ALL the others who've tried it throughout history. Or, they're not lazy at all and want to use Socialism as the means for taking away the wealth of others for their own gain.

If this sounds a bit harsh, it's here precisely written for that purpose. As soon as you start your own business, you join a unique community that produces most of the wealth for our country. At the same time you will be putting yourself in the line of fire that comes from all the blamers, doubters, malcontents, defeatists, criticizers and takers the world has to offer. You need to learn about this great system we have and be prepared to defend it against all the people who want to ruin it with their regulations and excessive taxation that they need for funding all their government give-away programs and to redistribute the country's wealth from those who have created it to those who are either unable or unwilling to create or work for their own wealth. There is a big difference between folks who are unable to create their own wealth and those who are busy trying to confiscate somebody else's wealth. Be ready to help those who need help and resist those who are TAKERS.

## The Common Criticisms

There are a few things that Free Enterprise is always criticized for that we have just enough limited space to cover in this particular publication:

1. The first criticism is that the Free Enterprise System creates distance between the rich and poor. That is only true if the poor don't try to lift themselves out of their poverty by taking advantage of what the system can provide. If they go to the government for their provision instead of working through the Free Enterprise System for its potential, they will surely stay in their poverty. We need for more and more people to take advantage of starting their own small businesses instead of becoming dependent on the government dole that only produces poor people.

2. Another area of criticism is the fact that there is risk involved in the pursuit of free enterprise. But risk is directly related to FREE markets. And, profit potential is directly related to the amount of risk: the more risk in a venture, the greater the profit potential. Yes, there is always the risk of failure, but there is also as a

direct result the potential for greater economic success. Profit is a reward to the risk-taker.

3. Another criticism is that there are economic cycles involved. There are times of plenty but there are also down turns, recessions and occasionally a depression. A FREE economic system will always move in cycles but a great deal of the downward pressure on growth cycles and the negative pressure in the world's economies is caused by government interference and over-regulation that produce uncertainty. The greatest cause of economic failure is UNCERTAINTY.

4. A fourth criticism is that business people only respond to profit which makes them greedy people. The fact is a FREE economy produces profits and the greater the profits are, the more that can be made available for charitable giving. The greatest source of giving in the country is the pool of capitalistic profit produced by successful privately owned businesses.

5. People who are owners of business are immoral. The truth is the opposite especially when the system is based on biblical principles of life and enterprise. Jesus talked extensively about money and property and contrary to popular belief, He wasn't telling everyone they should be poor.

The bottom line for this chapter is that we should be eager to join the ranks of small business people but quick to defend our system of Free Enterprise when it comes under attack, which is pretty much constantly. It would help to study about it so you can know what you've become a part of and why you want to stay there in the face of all the criticism you'll be hearing. Following is some basic information that you can refer to in the future from *The Social Studies Help Center.*[7]

## Basic Principles of Free Enterprise

Now, the U.S. economic system of free enterprise operates according to five main principles:

### 1. Freedom to Choose Our Own Business

In this country, the decision to go into a particular business is yours alone to make. You will decide what prices to charge and what your working hours are. Certain laws prohibit you from cheating or damaging your customers or other people. But in theory you will be left alone to run your business as you want.

### 2. Right to Own Private Property

Private property can be a parcel of land, a home, or a car or any other asset that is owned by an individual, a family or group. It differs from public property like a city hall, a park, or a highway which provide a government service for all citizens. In the U.S. economic system, the right of people to buy and sell private property is guaranteed by law. But generally people do not have the right to use

---

[7] http://www.socialstudieshelp.com/eco_Free_enterprise.htm

their private property to interfere with the property rights of others or to harm them in some way. There are of course exceptions in applying this basic principle according to local practice and legislation consistent with federal constitutional law.

## 3. Profit Motive

The main reason for starting a small business is to make money. You make profit by taking in more money than you spend. The amount of money left over after subtracting your business expenses from your business income is called your profit. In the free enterprise system, business firms try hard to keep costs down and increase their sales revenue. The better they succeed at this, the higher their profits will be. Economists describe the efforts by business firms to earn the greatest profits as the "profit motive" and you do NOT have to apologize if you're motivated to make profit. Since it is private, what you do with your profit is your private concern even though takers will be trying constantly to tell you what you should do with your personal profit. The fact is the government encourages small business formation so that there will be ongoing future sources of tax revenue and to pay for their grandiose programs.

## 4. Competition

Just as you are free to start your own small business, so is everybody else. The rivalry among sellers in the same field to attract consumer dollars is called competition. If your business is profitable, it is likely others will enter the same type of small business hoping to be as successful as you. They will be competing with you for the same customers. To win a share of the particular market segment you are operating in, other sellers may try to offer more and better services or at lower prices. Because of the pressure of competition, business firms must constantly try to provide the best services and create the best products at the lowest possible prices.

## 5. Sovereignty of the Customer

In the end, it is the customers, the consumers who determine whether any business succeeds or fails. In the U.S. free enterprise economy, consumers are said to have sovereignty which is the power or freedom to have final say. Consumers are free to spend their money for your products or somebody else's products. If they prefer somebody else over you, then your company may lose money, go out of business or decide to market some different product or service. And so, how consumers choose to spend their available dollars causes business firms of all kinds to produce certain goods and services and not others.

## Adopting a Code of Conduct

Many entrepreneurs assume that the morals of private enterprise will be automatically adjusted by forces in the marketplace. In other words consumers will eventually tend to gravitate away from immoral small businesses that profit by cheating consumers over to businesses that follow an ill-defined but acceptable Code of Conduct. But I differ with that view because I believe that the best system for anything in life will ALWAYS be based on a biblically-based model that depends upon honesty and deference to others. Even though this book isn't intended as a Christian-oriented book per se, I would be remiss if I didn't tell you that the system that will produce the greatest profitability for you long term is the FREE system of private capitalism that has incorporated a Christian, bible-based view of business.

The purpose of this book is to help you start and operate a small business but if you would like to know more about establishing your business with a Christian view, be sure to check out Chapters 12 and 13. Otherwise, you can skip those parts for now and come back to them someday when you're more interested in how it could help you. For the present just know that small business provides a wonderful opportunity for financial and personal success if you are fair to others and understand how the marketplace works based on the principles outlined in this publication.

# 4. Basic Guidelines for New Business Startups

A nyone who's considering the startup of a new business should think and pray and prepare long and hard about it before they make any irreversible decisions. Starting a new business is a major undertaking that requires a lot of hard work and sacrifice. Everybody should do it but not until they're prepared for it. Following here are some basic guidelines to consider:

1. Before taking any action, find out what God wants you to do. If He is leading you and you continue to follow His lead, success is assured. Remember: not everyone is necessarily destined to start his or her own business. Or if it is your destiny, it may be for a later time. Be content with what God has for your life but be sure about what He has for you to do NOW.

2. Try to set aside as much cash as possible to put into your new business. Ask God for supernatural provision. Keep in mind that a new business often requires a minimum of one year to get to the point of producing a positive cash flow. And during that time you'll have to live and provide for your family's needs. Remember: life's priorities should be God first and family second before anything else.

3. If you're presently working for someone else, <u>consider starting your new business from your home on a part</u>

time __basis__ working at it in the evenings and on week-
ends. In this way you can continue to enjoy the income
from the employer you work for while your new
company is becoming established. When you see that
your business can support your basic financial needs,
you can consider going into it on a full time basis.

4. __The most rapidly growing industry in the United States__
   __is home-based business__. There are thousands of
   publications on the Internet and in bookstores to help
   you start one. Once the business starts to grow and
   there's some cash flow, you can consider renting
   office space but keep in mind you'll be asked to sign a
   binding lease for typically at least one year. The
   landlord won't care if one day you can't pay the rent
   because your business didn't produce enough cash
   flow. In fact, he/she may pursue you in Court for any
   unpaid rent. There are office colonies available in
   virtually any real estate market in the country that
   offer a combination of adequate office space with
   administrative services that's often a good way to get
   started in an office at an affordable rent.

5. When you're considering what kind of business to go
   into, most people will want to pursue something that
   comes to them naturally, something they're already
   interested in. Many people convert hobbies into
   profit-generating businesses. If you've had a long-
   time interest in a particular product or service, it could
   be pointing you toward something to pursue in

business. People are more likely to succeed in business if they're working on something they're interested in and passionate about.

6. When you're considering a new business, find one that requires little or no startup capital (unless you've already accumulated the capital). If you need any significant amount of capital to start your new business, <u>the reality is that it's very difficult to find unsecured commercial loans for new ventures</u>. So, many people use credit cards and other means to generate unsecured loans and some even mortgage their homes to start their businesses. We strongly recommend <u>against</u> burdening a new business and yourself with bank debt. If you do need to incur a lot of startup debt, it would be a sign for many people that it's either the wrong time or the wrong type of business. *To borrow against one's home to start a new business is especially something to be avoided.*

7. There are plenty of service industry businesses that don't require significant amounts of working capital including real estate sales and management, mortgage broker, insurance sales, counseling, tutoring, child care, etc. Try to pursue a service concept related to your area of interest if your capital is short so you won't have to invest in an inventory of products.

8. When you start a new business, you do NOT have to incorporate immediately. Until you do incorporate, you will be operating as a sole proprietorship. However,

you WILL need to register a fictitious name (DBA) with your state so you can open a separate bank account in the name of your business. DBA is the common acronym for "Doing Business As." Please don't make the mistake even from the beginning of trying to pay both your personal and business expenses from the same bank account.

9. When you start a new business you should avoid 50/50 partnerships. They are historically more prone to failure than sole proprietorships because of disagreements between the partners. If there must be a partnership it should always be set up with the understanding that one of the partners has the authority to make final decisions and the other partner agrees and submits to that authority from the beginning. You could consider rotating the partner in authority on a periodic basis like from year to year.

Also, any partnership should have a dissolution agreement from the beginning to provide for the possibility that after a period of working together, the partners find they're not sufficiently compatible. The breakup can be triggered by a notice in writing from one partner to the other advising of the former's desire to dissolve the partnership in accordance with the terms of the Agreement.

Partnerships with family members only succeed by exception. Try to stay away from them! You can lose important relationships for life if things go wrong.

10. One of the biggest problems we see in small businesses is that entrepreneurs place all of their attention on the functional operations of their companies and almost none on the financial and administrative parts. Someone can be an expert in their chosen field and fail at it because their financial records and their offices are in total disarray. *In business, the first priority for the entrepreneur has to be the money.* If you don't take care of and account for the money, you'll probably fail even if you're an expert in the product or service you trying to sell. Before you ever start a serious business, figure out *how* you're going to account for the money.

Very often we talk to small business people who don't have a background or training in accounting or business economics and they feel lost when it comes to managing their money. Some don't yet possess even the basic financial skills that a business is going to require. The solutions to this are to find friends or family members who will help you until you learn, and to attend relevant community training courses so you can acquire the basic knowledge. *Please don't be in a rush to start your new business until you have this ground covered.* You must be able to read and understand the three basic financial statements of an ongoing business BEFORE you start your own.

11. Flowing from the problem of inattention to the money, another big problem we see is that small

business people have no idea what their ongoing profitability is and whether or not they're actually making any money. They tend to rely on the balance in their bank accounts at any point in time, which is a formula for disaster. You need to have a budget and <u>you need to know how you performed every month against your budget</u>. You also need to have an accountant or book keeper prepare a basic monthly *Income Statement* for you and you need to be able to understand and interpret it. And, you need to have access to it within the first few days of the following month so you'll have plenty of time to take action if you need to in response to whatever you find there.

12. Another typical problem is that most small business owners tend to take too much money out of their business for personal living expenses. When the bank account increases they take money out of the business without giving adequate consideration to upcoming cash requirements for operating expenses, replenishment of working capital, debt repayment and any other cash needs the company is going to have. A good idea is to put yourself on a fixed salary and include it in your monthly budget to avoid the tendency to overdraw. Anyway, you want to consistently take out less than the company makes so its capital/net worth can grow.

13. If you're collecting sales taxes and/or employee payroll taxes, you should place the related funds in a

separate bank account from the very beginning of your company. This money doesn't belong to you; you're collecting it in trust for government entities. We have seen businesses fail that unadvisedly or inadvertently used tax revenues in the operation of their companies and were unable to find sufficient cash later on when they came due. You must be organized enough to avoid mingling tax revenues with your operating revenues. Governments will NOT be merciful if you're unable to remit their money.

14. From the beginning of starting a new company, purpose to be organized. Maintain an orderly office and plan your time. Most small business people are tremendously disorganized (because they don't give enough attention to the administrative requirements of business) and they waste a lot of time in unproductive endeavor. Disorder and confusion are <u>never</u> God's way of doing things.

15. If eventually your company is able to hire employees, remember that you have a responsibility to help them succeed. In time, you may even find that some of them have become good candidates for imminent business ownership on their own in which case you have a responsibility to help them prepare and step out in faith. If you selfishly put yourself first and neglect the needs of your employees or if you're autocratic and dictatorial, experience shows that your business is likely to fail.

In sum, an employer has a special responsibility for discipling their employees and a lot of small businesses fail to embrace this important concept often leading to their unfortunate demise. The basis for this responsibility is biblical and biblical principles shouldn't be ignored.

Nevertheless, you should also watch how your employees handle your money. I have seen MANY instances where employees embezzled money. Be careful. Occasional audits are smart. Watch any Petty Cash to be sure you have receipts for all the cash that's going out. Just make is plain that you are careful with your money and watch over it. Hopefully, they will get the idea.

16.    Finally, keep in mind that most business these days requires some degree of computer and Internet savvy. This includes the social media which is increasingly vital for successful marketing in the modern marketplace. If you're a little techno-challenged, I suggest that you look for some free courses at local universities or empowerment ministries to increase your expertise. The more you know in this area the better off you'll be. You can't learn too much about this area of your business.

Follow these principles of small business operation and the probability of your success WILL increase. Of course, it's not a complete list but it's a really great start!

# MONTHLY BUSINESS BUDGET PERFORMANCE

Company Name: _____ Date: _____

| EXPENSE CATEGORIES | BUDGET | ACTUAL | YEAR TO DATE |
|---|---|---|---|
| Employee Salaries | | | |
| Payroll Taxes & Benefits | | | |
| Consultants | | | |
| Rent/Lease Payments | | | |
| Mortgage Payments | | | |
| Advertising/Promotions | | | |
| Websites | | | |
| Postage/Shipping | | | |
| Supplies | | | |
| Communications/Telephone | | | |
| Utilities | | | |
| Other Taxes | | | |
| Insurance | | | |
| Interest Expense | | | |
| Bank Service Charges | | | |
| Repairs & Maintenance | | | |
| Professional Services–Acctg | | | |
| Professional Services–Other | | | |
| Travel & Entertainment | | | |
| Miscellaneous | | | |
| | | | |
| Total Monthly Operating Costs | | | |

## (A TYPICAL BUDGET LAYOUT FOR SMALL BUSINESS)

# THE TEN MOST IMPORTANT OBSTACLES TO A SUCESSFUL BUSINESS <u>STARTUP</u>

1. The Owner lacks administrative preparation and knowledge.
2. The Owner makes a poor choice of his primary product or service to offer.
3. The Owner has inadequate startup capital.
4. The Owner invests too much in non-critical assets.
5. The Owner makes an emotional selection of the business location.
6. The Owner has no knowledge for how to attract prospective customers.
7. The Owner failed to seek advice from professionals: CPA, Legal, Insurance, etc.
8. The Owner made a poor choice of the business type: Sole Proprietor, S-Corp, etc.
9. The Owner has insufficient experience with the product or service being offered for sale.
10. The Owner started with insufficient prior planning and investigation.

# THE TEN MOST IMPORTANT OBSTACLES TO <u>RUNNING</u> A SUCESSFUL BUSINESS

1. The Owner failed to perform business planning including setting financial targets and goals.
2. The Owner had no knowledge of how to handle finances and records keeping.
3. The Owner did not invest enough of the available in inventory and employee payroll.
4. The Owner had poor credit granting practices.
5. The Owner priced products or services emotionally instead of making a competitive assessment and cost analysis.
6. The Owner took too much out of the business for personal living expenses.
7. The Owner tried to expand the business too rapidly and did not have enough capital available.
8. The Owner invested in advertising that was ineffective.
9. The Owner did not borrow enough to capitalize the business for the long term.
10. The Owner was delinquent in the payment of taxes and used the related money for other purposes.

**BE SURE TO DO YOUR RESEARCH**

# 5. Types of Organizations

One of the questions you'll face as you start forming your new business is which type of organization you should use. Many small businesses start out as Sole Proprietorships and then graduate into a more sophisticated form after the business has proven itself. They can also start out in one of the other forms depending upon the circumstances.

None of them is particularly difficult to put together and most cities have specialized business formation agencies that can help you including making the appropriate registrations with your state for a relatively modest fee. There are also Internet firms that provide this service. It's important to make the right decision on which one of the following main types of organizations to choose:

1. **Sole Proprietorship** = A sole proprietorship is a type of business entity that is owned and run by one individual and in which there's no legal distinction between the owner and the business.

   The owner receives all profits (subject to taxation specific to the business) and has unlimited responsibility for all losses and debts. Every asset of the business is owned by the proprietor and all debts of the business are the proprietor's. It is a "sole" proprietorship in contrast with *partnerships* involving more than one owner.

As a Sole Proprietor of a registered business, you will be able to deduct certain business expenses for the purpose of reducing the amount you pay for income taxes even though you're still on the payroll as an employee of a large company. This is why we recommend that everybody try to have a registered small business conducting at the least some simple ongoing enterprise that meets IRS requirements.

2. **General Partnership** = Partnerships involve a business organization formed between two or more people. All the members are known as partners and are joint owners of the entire business organization. Let's be clear about this type of organization: if at all possible avoid it and find another way to start your small business. Analyze it: why do you need a partner other than your spouse?

Nevertheless, if you decide on getting into one, the partners as a group are accountable for any profit, loss or liability of the business organization. An important step for this type of company is that all partners need to enter into a formal, pre-defined written agreement regarding profit sharing and loss bearing, before starting their venture.

Irrespective of the amount of capital brought in by each of the various partners or the profit-loss sharing percentage agreed on for each partner in what's called a *General Partnership*, any partner can be legally liable to pay off the TOTAL debts of the company if there's a problem in the future because the partners have *joint* liability. There is also *several* liability in other types of partnerships which mean that their obligation for paying the debts of the organization is proportional to the capital they have contributed. Finally, it's imperative to have a specific *Agreement of Dissolution* in the event one of the Partners wants to leave.

One thing that's often overlooked with Partnerships is that there must also be a mutual agreement dealing with how business decisions are made. There should always be one of the partners who has the authority to make the final decision for the business entity when the voting of the partners is tied. Many partnerships have failed because the partners couldn't agree on some particular issue or other and was no longer able to go forward for lack of a key business decision.

3. **C–Type Corporation** = A traditional Corporation (or a "C" Corporation) is a business structure that is created as a separate, distinct legal entity from its owners (also called "shareholders"). Once a corporation is formed, the corporation can have its own bank accounts, own property, conduct business, and even establish a line of credit distinctly separated from the individual accounts or credit of the shareholders. The primary advantage to having a business formed as a corporation is the fact that the shareholders are not necessarily personally liable for the debts and legal liabilities incurred by the corporation. For example, if

a corporation is sued for business reasons and loses, the shareholders will not be required to satisfy the debts of the corporation from their own personal assets (unless they have personally guaranteed those debts). This safeguards assets and properties of the individual shareholders, and as such, is more attractive to potential investors.

Once a corporation is established, the shareholders must name (via an election process) a board of directors that's responsible for the operation of the business, making business decisions, and managing all business-related activities. This board is elected by the shareholders of the corporation, and once named, the board appoints "officers" of the corporation to specific duties. This usually includes a secretary, a treasurer, etc.

Another important thing to know about the formation and maintenance of a corporation is that certain corporate formalities must be observed. These are things like a required annual meeting of the board of directors, the necessity to maintain the corporate "minutes," the separation of corporate and personal funds (no "co-mingling" of funds), and a necessity to maintain written agreements for all corporate transactions (including internal transactions such as internal loans, executive compensation agreements, etc.).

4. **S-Type Corporation** = The name "S-Corporation" comes from the fact that its organization meets the IRS requirements for taxation under *Subchapter S* of the IRS Tax Code. It's a corporation that is structured to provide a pass-through entity for tax purposes, much like a partnership whose income or losses "pass through" to the individual shareholders' personal tax returns (in direct proportion to their investment or ownership in the company), while still providing the same protections for assets and from liabilities as a traditional corporation. The shareholders will pay personal income taxes based on the S-Corporation's income, regardless of whether or not the income is actually distributed, but they will avoid the "double taxation" that has to be paid in connection with the traditional "C" Corporation which includes: (a) a tax must be paid on corporate profits plus (b) the shareholders pay tax on any dividend distributions they receive. The S-Type Corporation can be particularly attractive to the small family business where limited liability is a particular concern.

Most small businesses starting out will probably want to move quickly from the Sole Proprietorship organization to an S-corporation. Anyone who's still working as an employee of a big company can conduct their own S-type corporation as a side small business and take advantage of the business deductions the same as a Sole Proprietorship. Get some help from a

CPA to identify legal deductions that are available to small businesses.

5. **Limited Liability Company** = An LLC is a hybrid business entity having certain characteristics of both a corporation and a partnership. An LLC is a type of unincorporated association and is therefore not a corporation. The primary characteristic an LLC shares with a corporation is limited liability and the primary characteristic it shares with a partnership is the availability of pass-through income taxation. It is often more flexible than a corporation and can have a single owner.

LLC members are subject to the same liability protection as corporate shareholders. However, it's more difficult to pierce the LLC veil because LLCs don't have many formalities to maintain as corporations. So long as the LLC and its members don't commingle funds, it's difficult to pierce its veil. Membership interests in LLCs and partnership interests also have a significant level of protection through the charging order mechanism. The charging order limits the creditor of a debtor-partner or debtor-member to the debtor's share of distributions without conferring on the creditor any voting or management rights. LLC members may in certain circumstances also incur a personal liability in cases where distributions to members render the LLC insolvent.

To sum up, the purpose of this chapter is to introduce you to the knowledge that there are several kinds of organizations you can consider. Your best approach when you start your small business is to contact a CPA in order to receive current and direct advice on the type of organization you should choose in relation to specifically what you have in mind.

Nevertheless, you can start any small business almost immediately simply by registering a DBA in your state and opening a bank account. Then you can change later to another business type once you've become established.

Most people will wind up in an S-Corporation either from the start or later on after a time as a Sole Proprietor. Keep in mind that the formation of any corporation including an S-Type is a process that you'll probably need some help with. And, it requires a bit more administrative knowledge than a Sole Proprietorship.

To end this chapter, we want to emphasize the importance of establishing a good relationship with a CPA or an experienced business accountant. Do NOT try to cheap out on this because <u>we ALL need expert PROFESSIONAL advice to be successful</u>. Keep that in mind: you WILL need professional assistance and to try skipping it is a formula for disaster. Along with that, don't try to prepare your own business tax returns either. You won't do it correctly and you won't have time to learn what you need to know to do them correctly. PLEASE: never cheap out on the financial and administrative parts of your business!

# Relative Advantages and Disadvantages of Various Business Forms

| Issue | Sole Proprietor-ship | C Corp. | General / Limited Liability Partnership | Limited Partnership | Limited Liability Company | S Corp. |
|---|---|---|---|---|---|---|
| Self-employment Income from Entity | Yes | No | Yes | Yes -GP No -LP | Usually; See Proposed Regs§ 1.140-2(a)-18 | To extent of salary and bonus |
| Effect of Passive Loss Limitation Rules | N/A | Applies at corp. level/generally avoidable for larger corps. | Partners may or may not materially participate | Ltd. partners deemed not to materially participate | Members may or may not materially participate | Shareholders may or may not materially participate |
| Availability of Entity Losses to Owners | N/A | No | Flow through of losses to owners | Flow through of losses to owners | Flow through of losses to owners | Flow through of losses to owners |
| Fringe Benefits | Limited compared to C Corp | Widest available | Limited compared to C Corp | Limited compared to C Corp | Limited compared to C Corp | Limited compared to C Corp |
| Estate Planning Opportunities | Fair | Very good | Good | Very good | Very good | Fair |
| Accumulated Earnings and PHC Tax | N/A | Section 531 and Section 541 applicable | No | No | No | No |
| State Taxes | Same as individual | Generally uniform and deductible | Generally uniform | Generally uniform | States vary | States vary |
| Dividend Received Deduction | N/A | Allowed | Not allowed | Not allowed | Not allowed | Not allowed |
| Effect of Bus. Liabilities on Owner's Basis | Full effect | No effect | Proportionate share | Limited partners share in nonrecourse | Proportionate share | Only shareholder's own loans |
| Alternative Minimum Tax | Subject to AMT | Subject to corporate AMT | Preference items flow to each partner | Preference items flow to each member | Preference items flow to each member | Preference items flow to each shareholder |
| Method of Accounting | Cash method | Depends on size and ownership | Generally may use cash method | Generally may use cash method | Generally may use cash method unless farming syndicate | Generally may use cash method |

Source: Principles of Ag Law, Roger A. McEowen, Neil E. Harl

# 6. Basics of Writing a Business Plan

Every business needs a formal Business Plan even if you're not going to borrow money. And if you _are_ thinking about borrowing money, say to finance working capital for example, the first thing the bank will ask you for is your business plan. For small bank loans a simple three to five page Executive Summary of your Business Plan will usually be adequate for the typical small business and it should contain the basic information outlined at the end of this chapter.

If you want to get more sophisticated you can purchase software either on line or at your local office supply store. The related software purchase cost is on average about $150. There are also Business Plan provider/preparers including our own ministry with a normal cost at present of about $495 which includes ONGOING online access, mentoring and archiving. Our Business Plans can also uniquely interface with the QuickBooks Accounting system so the user can compare current performance against the Business Plan on an ongoing basis.

Other Business Plan providers charge $500–$750 not including online access nor ongoing mentoring nor the interface with QuickBooks. Here are a couple of websites outside our ministry (as of this writing) you can review:

www.businessplans.com
www.bizplaneasy.com

Having a Business Plan addresses the need to be organized but few small businesses do one. Most of the folks who DO are successful. The ones who are successful, like you want to be, can show you their Business Plans and they faithfully update them at least every year. Said another way, 90+% of small business failures don't have one. Your Plan doesn't have to be complicated either, so keep it simple and use it.

I also think it's very important for a small business to keep a close watch on a short list of near-term objectives. A good time to review your list of objectives is at the end of the year just before you start the new-year. Any objectives you didn't achieve in the previous year should be re-evaluated and either dropped or revised or retained and repeated for the coming operating period. I don't like to see organizations without a vibrant list of operating objectives with corresponding action plans that are under ongoing review and are constantly in motion.

If you decide to borrow funds for your company, the lender will want a detailed accounting of what you'll be using the funds for. They will also want to know how the loan will affect your operating performance. In other words, what will be the results of borrowing the money compared to not borrowing? If the indebtedness doesn't improve your operating performance over the next three years verses NOT borrowing the funds, then the lender will want to know why you want to borrow. Pointless indebtedness isn't something lenders want to consider.

When you borrow funds, you will need to have your financial statements ready as attachments to the Business Plan. The financial statements have to include an Income Statement and a Balance Sheet. The Income Statement should show the current year performance and a forecast for the next three years. You will also need tax returns for the previous two or three years both personal and business. On the Balance Sheet the lender is going to want to see some liquidity that could pay back a substantial portion of the debt if it became necessary.

If you are borrowing for a small company with a relatively limited amount of business assets, be prepared to have to personally guarantee the repayment of the debt. That's just the way it is and it means that if your small business fails, you will have to use personal assets to repay the outstanding debts of the business. Or, the business will have to seek protective re-organization through bankruptcy.

Another use for a Business Plan is for the purpose of attracting investors to provide additional capital for your business. Very often that type of Business Plan will be more detailed and you will need to be prepared to answer a lot of questions. You will also need to be prepared to give up equity in your company equivalent to taking in partners. I don't usually recommend soliciting investors who have to have an equity position in your company unless you can avoid having them participate in its management. By all means avoid that hassle if you can.

Most people think it's easy to borrow from the SBA (Small Business Administration). But it is NOT easy and involves a lengthy administrative process. If you are a new startup business, don't waste your time until you have at least 12 consecutive months of profitable operating performance. The SBA likes to see an established track record for young companies that are looking to expand.

When you do become a candidate for an SBA Loan, you will find a wealth of information in Appendix One of this publication that will help you apply for one. We can also assist you if the going gets tough. It's not an easy process.

In sum, a professionally prepared Business Plan serves three basic purposes:

1. It helps you get organized.
2. It provides essential information to prospective lenders.
3. It forms a basis for monitoring your operating performance.

In short, a Business Plan works like a financial plan or budget that will really help you be successful. Please don't ignore it because you might be sorry.

The following page shows a functional outline of a very basic Business Plan. You can start with it and graduate to one of our more sophisticated online plans later whenever you feel you're ready.

# BUSINESS PLAN

Name of Company: _____
Plan Date: _____

Contact Information:

Names and Addresses of Principals of the Business:

Description of the Business performed:

Basic Mission:

Principal Operating Objectives:

Financial Performance and Objectives:
    Last Year
    Current Year Forecast:
    Current Year +1:
    Current Year +2:

Current Year Operating Budget:
    Sales
    Cost of Goods Sold
    Gross Margin
    Operating Expenses
    Net Profit

Recommendations and Future Plans:

# 7. How to Build Startup Credit

Are you thinking about using credit to help finance your new business? You're not alone because statistics show that over 65% of all business owners use credit for things that have to be purchased by the business. But what's somewhat alarming about that is that only 50% of those credit accounts are actually in the name of the business. In other words, they are personal accounts in the name of the owner or a spouse.

As a business owner, using personal credit cards for business is a risky practice since you assume total liability personally. If your company is sued or fails financially, you risk losing personal assets and your good credit rating. So try to avoid it and do your best to NOT use your personal assets as collateral for business credit.

So how do you go about building credit in the company's name without putting your personal credit on the line? For starters, if you're already operating as a sole proprietorship, you'll need to incorporate your business so you can obtain a *Federal Tax Identification number*. It's often referred to as an EIN Number. If you're just starting up, then go directly to an S–Type Corporation and skip the sole proprietorship model.

As a corporation your company is treated as a separate entity with its own tax registration with the IRS and state agencies and it's totally separated from you personally. It files its own tax returns and it can also create its own credit lines completely separate from its owners. Banks will ask you for a personal guarantee for bank loans but what we're talking about in this section is building startup credit with either corporate credit cards or trade credit <u>so you can avoid bank loans</u>.

Your company's Tax ID Number aka *Employer Identi-fication Number (EIN)* is the number that you will use to register with the business credit bureaus including *Dun and Bradstreet, Credit Safe, Capital One Business, Experian, Equifax,* etc.

You will also be required to provide your EIN number on corporate credit applications because lenders use this information to conduct a business credit check on your company before deciding whether or not to extend a line of credit to it.

Before you start applying for credit, make sure your corporate records, state filings and required business licenses are all up to date. In addition, get your company's phone number listed in the 411 directory so a supplier or lender can complete every aspect of its verification during the underwriting process.

After that you should be ready to apply for credit and the best place to start is with your supplier-vendors. Many types of suppliers, including major brands, extend lines of credit to businesses like yours giving you the opportunity to finance inventory purchases and conserve your company's cash. You may start with a vendor with short-term credit say like 15 days, but with good experience most vendors will soon be open to the idea of extending your credit repayment term to longer periods like 30 or 60 days. And don't forget that most of your vendors have competitors who may be more than willing to extend credit terms to your company in order to win your business. Credit is often a good way to secure new business for them. And, when YOU give credit to your customers, use the related Accounts Receivable as collateral for bank loans and avoid a personal guarantee.

You should focus on applying for credit with suppliers that provide products and services your company needs regularly so that you can make the related purchases with your credit lines. You can usually obtain products like office supplies, computers and marketing materials with payment terms ranging from net 30 to net 60 days.

By paying all your invoices on time, you'll be building good business credit history which will increase your company's credit rating and make it possible to obtain additional financing as time goes on. Ask your vendors to be sure and report your good credit payment history to the commercial credit bureaus because they're the ones who assemble and publish the related credit reports.

With a strong business credit report you can stop relying on your personal guarantee for the financing that your company needs. Since a creditor, lender or supplier will be able to easily determine your company's risk level by contacting the commercial credit bureaus, qualifying for future credit will be an increasingly easier process.

As a new startup, it's certainly possible for you to decide on operating your business as a sole proprietorship and using your personal credit to fund your business simply because it's one of the easiest structures to create and you already have credit cards on hand. If you're operating your business as simply a tax shelter and you aren't interested in making it grow yet, you can consider staying as a sole proprietor.

But if you want to grow your business more quickly by building business credit, you can improve your company's image, protect your personal credit, limit your liability and increase your credit capacity since businesses once they're established can obtain typically 10 to 100 times greater financing then an individual.

## A Word of Caution

You will most likely discover that it's relatively easy to obtain credit for your company especially as time goes on and you demonstrate your ability to pay your bills on time. But there's a tremendous temptation in front of you which is getting too much credit. Many of the business failures racked up in the first five years of life are caused by obtaining more credit than the company can afford.

When banks evaluate companies as prospective borrowers, they will tend to look at various operating and financial ratios calculated from data you will provide them on your company's financial statements. One of the traditional ratios is called the *Current Ratio* and it's calculated as follows: current assets divided by current liabilities as reported on your company Balance Sheet. If the ratio is less than one, it indicates to the creditor that you don't have enough assets to pay off all your short-term debts. A ratio more than three might suggest to the bank that your company isn't being aggressive enough. Therefore, the traditional view for this ratio is that it should be more than one and perhaps not much greater than two. You accountant can provide you with this ratio on a monthly basis if you request it and you should use it just for a basic indication of the financial health of your company.

In addition, banks and accountants use a number of other ratios to evaluate the financial health of a business. Your accountant can educate you about the ones that are the most popular for the industry that your company is involved in and some related guidelines. But the basic concept is this: it's generally okay to increase your accounts payable to your vendors up to just BEFORE you have to start struggling to pay them ALL on time. If you have to start asking vendors for extended repayment terms, you've waited too long and acquired too much debt or you've experienced an unexpected financial hiccup that's telling you to start reducing accounts payable until you're not struggling anymore. Generally, you shouldn't owe more to your suppliers than you could pay off if you had to suddenly shut down your business tomorrow.

Another point to bring up in this section is that the tendency to over-borrow and have trouble paying creditors on time is often related to the owner-entrepreneur taking too much money out of the business for compensation USUALLY in combination with granting too much credit to the company's customers. How do we avoid these temptations?

First, you need to put yourself on a regular salary so that the company is *planning* for your compensation and then resist the temptation to take out additional money when you have an unexpected personal need that arises. What would you do if you were working for someone else and that personal need arose? You would probably use a personal credit card to take care of that need and then repay the credit card debt over a period of time from the ongoing compensation you're receiving from your employer. Get in the habit of working the same way with your own company.

The other big problem is the temptation to grant more credit to your customers than you can afford. Most entrepreneurs are way better sales people than they are administrators. They will do whatever's necessary to make a sale. But here's the problem: if you grant too much credit you won't have enough cash on hand when it comes to replenish your inventory or pay your ongoing operating bills! You made the sale but you don't benefit from it until you collect the payment from the customer and put the revenue back into your business.

These are some of the factors that lead to business failure. The moral of the story is this: JUST BE CAUTIOUS and don't overdo the indebtedness of your company! It can be a good thing to use other people's money but keep it where you can pay it off if you have to and don't be using other people's money to create a higher lifestyle for yourself. Debt is strictly for the purpose of helping your business grow and expand. Otherwise, AVOID IT!

Also, don't be in a hurry to give too much credit to make a sale. Find out what industry practices are for your type of business and stick to that guideline. If a customer starts having trouble paying you on time you need to be on top of that and be quick to reduce your exposure. Keep this in mind: it is ALWAYS better to NOT make a sale than to make a bad sale you can't collect on.

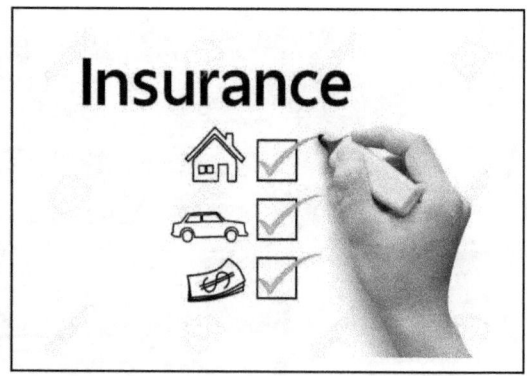

# 8. Other Essential Financial Issues

There are several other financial subjects we ought to go over before you go off to start your new business. Remember that I told you in an earlier chapter that the financial part of your new business will be the most important even though the operating part is more fun. I repeat it here and emphasize the following: YOU <u>MUST</u> AGGRESSIVELY PURSUE A BASIC UNDER-STANDING OF THE FINANCIAL PART OF YOUR BUSINESS.

## Accounting

The first subject is the importance of keeping your accounting up to date. In the beginning you can make the entries yourself and then later on hire a bookkeeper to keep things up to date. It's very important to do this as you go along so you don't come to the end of a tax year with a cardboard box full of papers and receipts that you'll have to pay someone to get organized for you.

I personally like the *Intuit Quick Books* accounting system because it can fit almost any business scenario. You will probably need some instruction but there are plenty of community workshops you can attend, and also QB has some tutorials that will teach you the principles of basic accounting. You CAN do this if you can learn to enter simple income and expense items and from there the system will pretty much take care of itself for entry level accounting. But you must have somebody on top of this part of your business so it's kept up to date monthly.

I also like the online version of QB because it's ongoing, your historical information is readily available and it's all backed up on QB servers. The other advantage of QB online is that it updates automatically so you don't have to buy the updates every year. The only downside is that you will have to pay a monthly user fee of about $25 to $30 but it's really worth it. If you get a CPA to open your account for you as one of their clients, you will probably get to enjoy a substantial discount.

Before leaving this section I want to leave you with a couple of accounting basics. The first is that a successful small business needs three principal financial statements.

### Income Statement

The first is an *Income Statement* containing the following major categories:

- *Sales Revenue*
- *Less Cost of the products sold (aka Direct Costs)*
- *Equals Gross Revenue*
- *Less Operating Expenses*
- *Equals Net Profit before Taxes*

An *Income Statement* tells you from month-to-month whether or not you're making any money. Most small business people have no idea. They can tell you everything about sales and nothing about finances. You need to know on an urgent ongoing basis whether or not your business is profitable. Otherwise you'll probably fail.

## Balance Sheet

The second major financial statement is called a *Balance Sheet*. It is called that because the value of every business is evaluated by two equal sides of an equation:

*Total Assets = Liabilities + New Worth*

The *Balance Sheet* tells the user the value of your company on the date it's prepared. The value of your business is called its *Net Worth*. It's also important to look at this financial statement over a period of several years to determine the trend. Is the *Net Worth* of your small business trending up or down? If it's going down it tells the user that your liabilities are increasing faster than your assets which could be an unhealthy trend.

## Cash Flow Statement

The third major financial statement is called a *Cash Flow Statement*. Its primary purpose is to provide information about a company's cash receipts and cash payments. Cash flow is NOT the same as net income; it's about the movement of money into and out of your company. The cash flow statement reports the cash provided and used by the operating, investing, and financing activities of a company during a particular accounting period. Information used to prepare a cash statement is taken from the income statement for the current year and balance sheets for the past two years.[8]

---

[8] https://www.zionsbank.com/pdfs/biz_resources_book-4.pdf

At the end of this chapter you'll find UNRELATED examples of these three financial statements. Study until you understand them. Most small business owners do NOT understand these business basics which is the main reason why 75% of them will fail before they're five years old. In other words, Small Business owners keep trying to be lazy and uninformed about small business financial administration and it doesn't work out 75% of the time.

## Taxes

I also want to emphasize the importance of keeping your taxes up to date because I continually run across self-employed entrepreneurs who're behind in filing their tax returns. Please don't do that! You have a LEGAL obligation to be current and orderly about the reporting and payment of your taxes. Render unto Caesar what is Caesar's and be glad that you made enough income that you owe a few tax dollars. And, NEVER allow yourself to get behind in the filing of your returns. Even if something happens and you don't have enough money for the moment to pay the tax you owe, it's usually better to go ahead and file your returns and send the related payment later with a little interest added on.

Most small business people will have a Form 1040 to file that summarizes personal income plus a Form 1120 for your S-corporation or the appropriate form for whatever business entity you finally adopted. If you collect Sales Tax, you will have to file and pay those tax receipts according to the procedures established in your state which is usually a monthly filing. If you have employees you will have to collect and account for the related payroll taxes. Or you can hire independent contractors and avoid the payroll tax situation. But, you will have to find out about the law and whether or not the people in your situation fit the legal profile for independent contractors.

When you start making some money, you really should hire an experienced tax accountant. Many of them have bookkeeping services so that your accountant can handle both requirements for you. They will keep track for you of when you have to file which tax return. It is unfortunate that taxes in our country have become so complicated but they are and you will need an expert. Do NOT begrudge the dollars you pay your accountant because he or she is performing a critical service that you are most likely NOT qualified to fully carry out on your own.

Now the idea of starting a small business in order to reduce you tax bill is so important that you'll find it discussed separately in a later chapter. The idea is that everyone should own a small business for the purpose of tax optimization.

## Insurance

Finally, resist the temptation to be underinsured. If you employ trade workers, go ahead and pay your Workmen's Comp Insurance and don't try to cheap out on your people. You also need liability insurance, coverage on the risk on any inventory you are holding, insurance on your vehicles, medical insurance, etc. Many small business people carry an umbrella policy that provides an array of different coverages with one policy. Consult your insurance professional to find out the best solutions for your particular needs.

If you have a family you should also look into two types of special insurance coverage: one is called Key Man Insurance which would provide your family with income if you are temporarily unable to work in your business and the income you get from it is dependent on your ability to work. A related kind of insurance is Disability Insurance which provides income to your family if you are seriously disabled for an extended period of time and have to hire someone to take over your responsibilities.

Don't forget to have a generous life insurance policy with a payout on your life of at least ten times your annual earnings. Term insurance is okay especially if you're still young. But you should also try to save some of your profit and invest it into low-risk growth instruments that will help you safely increase the value of your estate over an extended period of time. Consult a qualified life insurance agent or estate planner for guidance.

In conclusion, the success or failure of a business is almost always financial. It can fail for various reasons but the failure is ALWAYS a financial conclusion. Therefore, it makes sense to pay attention to the financial condition of your company. You neglect it at your own risk.

# EXAMPLE OF A TYPICAL SMALL BUSINESS INCOME STATEMENT

**Period Covered:** _____

|        |                            |    |           |        |
|--------|----------------------------|----|-----------|--------|
|        | Total revenue              | $  | 1,000,000 | 100%   |
| Less   | Cost of Goods Sold         | $  | 426,200   | 42.6%  |
|        | **Gross Profit**           | $  | **573,800** | 57.4% |
|        |                            |    |           |        |
| **Less** | **Operating Expenses**   |    |           |        |
|        | Accounting and legal fees  | $  | 11,700    |        |
|        | Advertising                | $  | 15,000    |        |
|        | Depreciation               | $  | 38,000    |        |
|        | Electricity                | $  | 2,700     |        |
|        | Insurance                  | $  | 15,200    |        |
|        | Interest and bank charges  | $  | 27,300    |        |
|        | Postage                    | $  | 1,500     |        |
|        | Printing and stationery    | $  | 8,700     |        |
|        | Professional memberships   | $  | 1,800     |        |
|        | Rent for premises          | $  | 74,300    |        |
|        | Repairs and maintenance    | $  | 21,100    |        |
|        | Training                   | $  | 6,900     |        |
|        | Vehicle operating costs    | $  | 20,000    |        |
|        | Wages and salaries         | $  | 223,500   |        |
|        | Workers compensation       | $  | 6,500     |        |
|        | All other expenses         | $  | 14,100    |        |
|        |                            |    |           |        |
| **Less** | **Total Operating Expenses** | $ | 488,300 | **48.8%** |
|        |                            |    |           |        |
| **Equals** | **Net Profit**           | $  | **85,500** | **8.6%** |

# EXAMPLE OF A TYPICAL SMALL BUSINESS BALANCE SHEET

Date _____

**ASSETS**

**Current Assets**

| | | |
|---|---|---|
| Cash | $ | 20,000 |
| Accounts receivable | $ | 15,000 |
| Inventory | $ | 150,000 |
| *Total Current Assets* | **$** | **185,000** |

**Non-Current Assets**

| | | |
|---|---|---|
| Plant and equipment | $ | 50,000 |
| Business premises | $ | 650,000 |
| Vehicles | $ | 70,000 |
| **Total Non-Current Assets** | **$** | **770,000** |

| | | |
|---|---|---|
| **TOTAL ASSETS** | **$** | **955,000** |

**Current Liabilities**

| | | |
|---|---|---|
| Accounts payable | $ | 25,000 |
| Bank overdraft | $ | 10,000 |
| Credit card debt | $ | 5,000 |
| Tax liability | $ | 30,000 |
| *Total Current Liabilities* | **$** | **70,000** |

**Non-Current Liabilities**

| | | |
|---|---|---|
| Long term business loan 1 | $ | 450,000 |
| Long term business loan 2 | $ | 50,000 |
| *Total Non-Current Liabilities* | **$** | **500,000** |

| | | |
|---|---|---|
| **TOTAL LIABILITIES** | **$** | **570,000** |
| **NET ASSETS** | **$** | **385,000** |
| **OWNERS EQUITY** | **$** | **385,000** |

# EXAMPLE OF A TYPICAL SMALL BUSINESS CASH FLOW STATEMENT

**Period Covered**_____

| | |
|---|---:|
| Cash flows from operating activities: | |
| Net income | $ 145,000 |
| Adjustments to reconcile net income to net cash provided by operating activities: | |
| Depreciation expense | 9,000 |
| Loss on sale of equipment | 3,000 |
| Decrease in accounts receivable | 10,000 |
| Increase in inventory | (5,000) |
| Increase in prepaid expenses | (4,000) |
| Increase in accounts payable | 16,000 |
| Decrease in income taxes payable | (2,000) |
| Net cash provided by operating activities | 172,000 |
| Cash flows from investing activities: | |
| Purchase of building | (120,000) |
| Purchase of equipment | (25,000) |
| Sale of equipment | 4,000 |
| Net cash used by investing activities | (141,000) |
| Cash flows from financing activities: | |
| Issuance of common stock | 20,000 |
| Payment of cash dividends | (29,000) |
| Net cash used by financing activities | (9,000) |
| Net increase in cash | 22,000 |
| Cash at beginning of period | 33,000 |
| Cash at end of period | $ 55,000 |

# 9. Designing a Marketing Plan

The second most important reason small businesses fail is because they lack a comprehensive marketing plan. The truth is, most small business owners don't have a clear idea of what MARKETING actually is which would explain why they don't plan for it. Consequently, most small business marketing is hap-hazard, ill-planned, defensive and dis-organized, lacking in specific goals and objectives for the company's bottom line.

The textbook definition of the word *marketing* is traditionally something like the following: *Marketing is all of the commercial activities involved in the transferring of goods and services from producer to consumer including the receipt of payment from the consumer.*

Once you move from the college textbook to the practicality of the small business genre, you're more likely to find a definition that looks like this: *Marketing activities and strategies result in making products and services available that satisfy customers while making profits for the companies that are offering those products and services.*

We've also seen the following definition which seems to reduce the definition down to the bare essentials that everybody can identify with: *Marketing is getting someone, who has a need, to know, like and trust you well enough to purchase your product or service.*

Trying to define the word MARKETING is something that writers and teachers have been playing with for generations. Put them all together and get the essence out of all of them because it's something you REALLY need to give priority to. Here are the basic questions the small business owner MUST answer that have to do with MARKETING before starting a new business:

- Where is the marketplace to sell my product (or service)?
- What is the competition doing in that marketplace and what can I do better?
- Who are my prospective customers?
- How will I let people know about my product?
- What are the benefits my product makes available?
- How will I convince people they need the benefits of my products?
- How much will it cost each month to communicate to my prospective customers?
- How much should I charge for my products?
- What kind of credit terms should I offer based on competitive practice in my marketplace?

## Creating a Marketing Plan

Firms that are successful in marketing almost always start with a good marketing plan. Large companies have plans with hundreds of pages; small companies can get by with a half-dozen. Put your marketing plan into a three-ring binder and refer to it monthly. Leave a tab for putting in monthly reports on sales/manufacturing. This will allow you to track performance as you carry out your Marketing Plan.

The plan should cover one year. For small companies, this is often the best way to think about marketing: things change, people leave, markets evolve and customers come and go. Later on we suggest creating a section of your plan that addresses the medium-term future two to four years down the road. But most of your plan should focus on the coming year.

You should allow yourself a couple of months to write the plan even if it's only a few pages. Developing the plan is the toughest part of marketing. And, while executing the plan has its challenges, deciding what to do and how to do it are the greatest challenges in marketing. Most marketing plans kick off on the first of the year or with the opening of your fiscal year if it's a different date.

Who should see your plan? All the players in your company should see it and be able to refer to it. Firms typically keep their marketing plans private for one of two very different reasons: Either they're too skimpy and management would be embarrassed to have them see it, or they're solid and packed with strategies that would make them valuable to competition.

You can't do a marketing plan without getting many people involved. No matter what your size, get feedback from all parts of your company: finance, manufacturing, personnel, supply and so on. This is especially important because it will take everybody in your company to make your marketing plan work. Your key people can provide realistic input on what's achievable and how your goals can be reached, and they can share any insights they have on any potential, as-yet-unrealized marketing opportunities, adding another dimension to your plan. If you're essentially a one-person management operation, you'll have to wear all your hats at the same time, but <u>at least the meetings will be short</u>!

## Things to Include in Your Plan

Marketing is essentially about communicating to consumers in such a way that you draw consumers to your products and services so you can show them the benefits and motivate them to make a purchase. The truth is, you aren't actually selling a product or service; rather, you're selling the BENEFITS that your product or service will provide to prospective clients. The objective is to convince your prospects they will enjoy the benefits if they make the purchase and that they can trust you and your company to deliver on what you have claimed. They must also be convinced that you can make better benefits available than your competition and that the benefits are worth the cost you are asking them to pay you.

Here are some of the things you are going to have to put into your marketing plan, consistent with the amount of money you have available, in order to provide the level of convincing communication you'll need to make in order to achieve your sales objectives:

Business Cards
Brochures
Market Analysis
Website
Blog Site
Advertising Budget
- Media
- Internet
Promotional Budget
Social Media
Sales Commissions
Donations
Community Organizations
Transportation
- Related to Sales
- Related to Product Deliveries
Industry Meetings
Ongoing Education
- Required for Licensing
- Voluntary to Increase Knowledge
Entertainment
Travel-Sales Related

In the beginning you probably won't need to establish such a detailed budget that would include all these categories but eventually let's hope you'll soon be successful enough that you will be instructing your staff to budget these items for the coming year and then manage your company according to the established budget. I have seen many companies go under because they spent too much money from their Operating Cash Flow for marketing activities and wound up with insufficient cash when it came time to replenish inventory.

Establish a budget and monitor your ongoing performance to avoid overspending. This is where small businesses need to identify with the example of the large companies. Budgets are well worth the effort!

# 10. How to Best Minimize Personal Indebtedness

Now there is one particular piece of financial advice that deserves one whole chapter. The truth is this: you'll NOT get very far owning your own business if you put yourself in a lot of PERSONAL debt. You should avoid it like the plague and endeavor to pay everything off every month. Even in your business don't just get married to some credit line with an ongoing long-term balance paying only the interest every month. Before you know it that balance will become a permanent problem. Pay off your debts as soon as you can, ALWAYS.

If you're already in some amount of PERSONAL debt I want to counsel you in the remainder of this chapter about what you need to know to get out of it in the shortest possible time.

In order to be successful in implementing a Debt Elimination Plan, you need to be determined and you need to follow a *structured strategy*. Most people just try to throw money at their indebtedness without having a real plan that's based on sound reasoning. You need to implement YOUR reduction plan following certain steps that almost always work. You must be organized, you must be persistent, you must be consistent and you can't let anything hinder you from obtaining your ultimate objective. If you're fed up with indebtedness, if you're tired of always being restricted financially from what you want to do then you're about ready to go forward with this program.

## Follow a Structured Strategy:

**Step 1**: Make an IRREVERSIBLE decision for your family that you're going to make a change and that you're going to follow your plan no matter what happens until you get out of debt. You must first decide to do something and take action before you can actually do it! But the decision to do it needs to be irreversible in the sense that you've made the decision not ever to go back to where you were. No going back! The decision has been made and you and your family are committed.

**Step 2**: Conduct a family meeting and get everyone on the same page. All the members of your family need to be in agreement with what you've decided to do and what your ultimate objective is. Make debt repayment a top priority for your WHOLE family. You need everyone involved, everyone committed to supporting your debt repayment plan. The entire family will have to make sacrifices until your objectives have been achieved and you need to be in agreement.

A good idea is to set up a procedure for resolving expenditure questions when they arise. From the beginning of the plan's implementation everybody should be in agreement on the procedure and how it will be used when these questions arise. Suppose one family member wants to spend money on something and the alternative is to apply that extra cash to your debt repayment plan. How will you resolve it without straining relationships? How will you be consistent when these questions keep coming up over the life of your program? You need a resolution procedure and you should agree from the beginning on how you'll use it.

And it's good to have children involved in the program too, even small children so that everybody is on board and totally supportive of the family project.

**Step 3:** The next step is to take the time to prepare a Family Budget. A simple form has been provided for your use at the end of this publication. Did you know that more than 85% of all American families have NEVER had a Family Budget? As the money comes it's spent according to a loose priority list that leaves open the family's optional expenses are going to be paid for. This is why most families run out of cash around the 21st of the month and have to put the rest of the month's expenses on credit cards. They have no idea or plan for how they're going to spend their money and so they just spend it until it runs out.

In order for this program to work you'll HAVE to have some form of Family Budget because part of the plan is to identify the amount of SURPLUS cash you're going to have available at the end of the month to apply to your debt repayment in the manner revealed in this publication. If you find yourself needing help in putting your Family Budget together, we recommend that you purchase one of our other publications, which provides a lot of detailed information about budgeting.

**Step 4:** From the outset of your program, you need to STOP using credit cards and STOP acquiring new debt. Cut those credit cards up if you have to and throw away the pieces! If you run short of cash during the month, do your best to find it in some other place in your Family Budget instead of using credit. If you don't stop acquiring new indebtedness, then you'll just be replacing the old debts with new ones. And you'll have less cash available to pay down your already existing debts because you'll be making new minimum payments on the new debt you've been acquiring. THIS PROGRAM CANNOT SUCCEED IF YOU DON'T STOP ACQUIRING NEW DEBT. Please take this step.

**Step 5:** As soon as possible put together a contingency fund of at least $2,000.00 before you start trying to get into your debt repayment program. If you get started in the repayment program too soon and an unexpected emergency strikes, it will be really discouraging to have to go back and take some of your old debt back to cover the problem. Having a contingency fund of this size can help you avoid that kind of dilemma. You will want to have those funds set aside in some kind of account that you can't access too easily and it should be a real emergency that causes you to go into your contingency.

Ultimately you will want to be saving for a much larger contingency fund as you're able of at least 6 months gross income and after that you should be working to put together a fully funded contingency fund of at least $100,000.00. That's one hundred thousand dollars! If you don't have debt payments every month you'll be surprised at how fast you can accumulate such a meaningful savings. Once you have it you'll probably never miss sleep again.

**Step 6:** Next you'll want to gather all your bills together. Find the most recent statement for each creditor that you won't be able to pay off at the end of the current month. Then arrange those statements starting with the lowest balance on top and going through all your creditors in the order of ascending outstanding balance until you reach the creditor with the highest outstanding balance at the end. For most families the creditor with the highest outstanding balance will be their home mortgage. To clarify: arrange all your debts from lowest outstanding balance at the top of the list to highest outstanding balance at the bottom.

On a piece of paper list your creditors from lowest outstanding balance to the highest. Indicate the creditor name, the current outstanding balance and the related monthly minimum payment. Section 3 has a table showing a typical scenario. This list will be the launch pad for your Accelerated Debt Repayment Plan

**Step 7:** Before you start the plan, pull your credit reports from the three national credit bureaus: Equifax, Experian and Trans Union. According to federal law you are entitled to receive one free credit report from each of the credit bureaus each year. To obtain your free annual credit report go to the following web site: **www.annualcreditreport.com**. You can order all three credit bureaus from this one web site.

The reason for ordering your credit reports is to be sure that you are including all your creditors in your debt reduction program. Sometimes people forget about older debts and will neglect to include them in the program. But your credit reports are likely to include everything up to seven years from the date of last activity. Don't forget to check the credit reports of both husband and wife because sometimes you can find a surprise where you didn't expect it. By the way, did you know that it's estimated that more than 70% of all credit reports contain errors? If your reports have any, you'll want to begin a correction process because as you go through your debt reduction program, you'll want to see improvement in your FICO Scores so you can obtain lower interest rates on your remaining debts and shorten the term of your repayment.

**Step 8:** Last, call each of your creditors and ask them to reduce your current interest rate to the lowest possible level. Many people who've made their payments on time and have generally a good payment history are paying interest rates higher than they have to because they haven't paid attention. Many Creditors will work with you and reduce your interest rate on a provisional basis but you have to request a reduction. If you make your payments on time for the next several months, they'll then consider another reduction. The point is though consumers have to be attentive and be proactive about their credit matters. You don't have to be afraid of your creditors. Tell them what you want and see what happens. The worst that could happen is that your creditor refuses to reduce your interest rate. But some of them WILL respond to your request and that could shorten your repayment program substantially because more of your monthly payments will be going to pay off principle. It's definitely worth a try!

If you feel the least bit intimidated by contacting your creditors, we recommend that you consider purchasing one of our other publications, which provides a lot of detailed information about how to deal with creditors. Just look for the following title in the publication list of Make a Way Ministries:

*How to Work with Creditors Yourself When You're Facing a Payment Problem*

Now you're ready to get started with your program. Take control of your finances, implement your repayment plan and stay on top of things. You'll be seeing substantial progress in no time!

## Use the Low Balance Accelerator Approach

The key getting out of debt in the shortest possible time is to put the maximum amount of surplus cash into the program. Therefore, when you prepare your Family Budget form, you'll want to be tough and frugal in calculating the maximum amount of Surplus Cash you have left over after paying for all your living expenses. Look for money everywhere! You must be able to come up with a positive number for the Surplus Cash Calculation in order to get out of debt with this program.

Next, take the list of creditors and outstanding balances that you prepared above in Step 5 and add up all the monthly minimum payments. Then subtract the total of the monthly payment minimums from the available **Surplus Cash** that you derived from the preparation of your Family Budget. The resulting number is called the **Accelerator**.

Next, review your list of outstanding debts which you previously arranged starting with the one with the lowest balance and proceeding through the list to the creditor with the highest outstanding balance at the bottom of the list. Please see the Typical Example shown at the end of this section to help guide you through this exercise.
Your first objective is to ATTACK the debt with the lowest balance and pay it off first as explained below and then afterwards descending down the list as you pay off each creditor with the lowest balance.

As the final step, add the full **Accelerator** amount to the monthly minimum payment at the top of the priority list and do that every month until it's paid off. The top of the priority list is the one with the LOWEST outstanding balance. All the other bills receive just their normal minimum monthly payments.

When the top priority bill is paid off, i.e. the one with the lowest balance, calculate a new **Accelerator** by adding the monthly minimum of the bill you've just paid off to the old **Accelerator**. Then move this new **Accelerator** down to the second bill on the priority list adding it to the normal minimum payment you're already paying. Continue moving down the list in this manner applying an increasing **Accelerator** to each monthly minimum until the entire list of debts, INCLUDING YOUR MORTGAGE, has been totally paid off. If you ever receive extra money for something, always pay down the creditor with the lowest balance.

Using this approach you won't care which accounts have the highest interest rates because there's no significant difference in the repayment time between this approach and one that features a prioritization by interest rates. When we run the two different approaches through the computer, they always come out about the same. The advantage of the approach based on lowest outstanding balance is that you'll begin to see progress earlier which motivates most families to push through to victory.

That's the main reason we recommend it over the approach based on interest rates.

On the following pages you'll find an example of a simple accelerated repayment plan covering seven unsecured creditors. The secured debts (the mortgage on the home and the car note) have been included at the end of the list. This is a fairly typical example both in the number of creditors and the amount that the family is in debt. Please be sure to study the comments that follow the numbers until you're sure you understand how it works.

Then you're ready to design your own program. Make a list of all your creditors from lowest balance to highest and go for it!

## Typical Example:

| Creditor | Balance | Min Mo Payment |
|---|---|---|
| Discover | 1,050 | 21 |
| Sears | 2,250 | 50 |
| Citibank | 3,000 | 68 |
| Chase | 3,500 | 70 |
| Amex | 4,200 | 84 |
| Bank One | 5,600 | 112 |
| Capital One | 6,100 | 183 |
| Sub Total Unsecured | 25,760 | 588 |
| | | |
| GMAC Auto | 17,125 | 350 |
| First Mortgage | 153,200 | 1,250 |
| | | |
| **TOTALS** | **$196,025** | **$ 2,188** |

## EXPLANATIONS:

- Surplus Cash from Budget = 650 (before payments to unsecured creditors)
- Accelerator = 650 – 588 = 62 per month
- Accelerator should be added to the minimum payment at the top of the Priority list only
- Payment to Discover = 21 + 62 = 83 per month
- All other payments remain the same (i.e. pay only the minimum monthly payments) until Discover is paid off
- Then payment to Sears = 50 + 83 = 133 per month until paid off
- Then payment to Citibank = 68 + 133 = 201 per month until paid off, etc.

# MONTHLY FAMILY BUDGET

## INCOME

| | Husband | | Wife |
|---|---|---|---|
| Gross Wages | ☐ | | ☐ |
| Net Wages | ☐ | | ☐ |
| 1099 Earnings | ☐ | | ☐ |
| Other Investments | ☐ | | ☐ |
| Alimony/Child Spt. | ☐ | | ☐ |
| Pension/Soc. Sec. | ☐ | | ☐ |
| Other | ☐ | | ☐ |

## EXPENSES

| | | | |
|---|---|---|---|
| Tithe/Donation | ☐ | Groceries | ☐ |
| Rent (incl. storage) | ☐ | Lunches | ☐ |
| Mortgage | ☐ | All Phones | ☐ |
| 2nd Mtg/Equity Loan | ☐ | Internet | ☐ |
| Property Taxes | ☐ | TV/Cable | ☐ |
| Property Insurance | ☐ | Car Payment (1) | ☐ |
| Condo/HOA Fees | ☐ | Car Payment (2) | ☐ |
| Electricity/Gas | ☐ | Auto Insurance | ☐ |
| Water/Sewer/Garbage | ☐ | Auto Repair/Oil | ☐ |

| | | | |
|---|---|---|---|
| **Gasoline/Tolls** | ☐ | **Clubs/Hobbies** | ☐ |
| **Vacation Lodging** | ☐ | **Subscriptions** | ☐ |
| **Ticket/Fare/Travel** | ☐ | **Tobacco** | ☐ |
| **Clothing** | ☐ | **Gifts** | ☐ |
| **Health Insurance** | ☐ | **Cleaning/Laundry** | ☐ |
| **Doctor/Dentist** | ☐ | **Hair/Person Care** | ☐ |
| **Meds/Vitamins** | ☐ | **Pet Care** | ☐ |
| **School Tuition** | ☐ | **Alimony/Child Spt.** | ☐ |
| **Books** | ☐ | **Life Insurance** | ☐ |
| **Child Care** | ☐ | **Savings/Investing** | ☐ |
| **Entertainment/ Dining** | ☐ | **Misc/Other** | ☐ |

- Property Taxes and Homeowners Insurance should not be itemized if the mortgage payment includes the related escrows. If the mortgage payment does not cover taxes and insurance, those costs must be itemized where provided by dividing the annual total by 12 to equal a monthly allocation.

- Items such as car repairs, vacations, clothes and gift expenses can be calculated by dividing the annual total by 12 to equal a monthly allocation.

TOTAL COMBINED INCOME =  ☐

TOTAL EXPENSES =  ☐

AVAILABLE SURPLUS TO PAY DEBT =  ☐

# Considerations for Your Personal Credit Reports

As you pay off your accounts you'll need to be aware of the effects of this program on your credit reports. It would be normal to assume that as you pay off your accounts it would be GOOD for your credit reports and increase all your FICO Scores. Well, it depends and that's why we've included this section in this publication. You'll need excellent FICO Scores if you ever need an emergency short-term loan.

First of all as you pay off an account your natural tendency will be to close the account even though you've hopefully put the related credit card somewhere out of your reach. But wait a minute: if the account you want to close is an older line of credit, older than say 3 or 4 years, it will be better for your credit scores to keep the account open with a zero balance. Having older lines of credit that are well managed are GOOD for your FICO Scores.

If you want to close something, close the newer accounts first. The lines of credit you obtained within the last 2 years or so can be closed first and you can save the older accounts for later. For closing accounts you want to have a gradual approach closing open accounts slowly over time working from newest to oldest. At the end of the program you should wind up with at least 3 open accounts, the older the better. Why 3 accounts? Because if you ever want to obtain a home mortgage the Lender is going to want to see at least 3 active trade lines on your credit reports in order to qualify you for the mortgage. In sum, don't overdo it. We're working under a flawed financial system so we need to be shrewd to make the best of it.

Another thing you should know is that it's good for your FICO to use your trade lines frequently. The trick is to know how to do that without getting into debt again. What you do is charge something on your credit cards during the month but pay it off totally at the end of the month. The credit reports will soon show the activity and as long as the outstanding balance is never greater than 40% of the account credit limit, the better your credit rating will be. In other words, it's better for your FICO Scores to show a little credit activity going through your open accounts than no activity at all. The fact that you're paying them off at the end of the month isn't reflected on your credit reports. If your credit reports show that you're operating with small balances in your open accounts, the computer models that determine the FICO Scores will interpret that as well-managed indebtedness which results in higher scores than no credit activity at all.

If any of your debts were settled for less than the outstanding balance of record, you will need to obtain a Satisfaction Letter from your Creditor that you can send to the Credit Bureaus to document your repayment. Satisfaction Letters should be obtained from the creditor BEFORE you pay the amount of the settlement. When you're dealing with creditors everything should be in writing. If you have any concerns about Debt Settlements, contact the Ministry office for advice: (800) 357-4223.

Also you may want to consider purchasing one of our other publications that deals with the task of improving your credit rating. Just look for the following title on Amazon.com:

### *Credit Repair that Reduces Monthly Payments*

If you find yourself needing help in putting your Family Budget together, we recommend that you purchase one of our other publications, which provides a lot of detailed information about budgeting. Just look for the following title at Amazon.com:

### *Budgeting Yourself to Financial Victory*

These publications have been successfully used for many years and can be a big help for most families. They are also not very expensive! If you don't like them, send them back to us for a full refund.

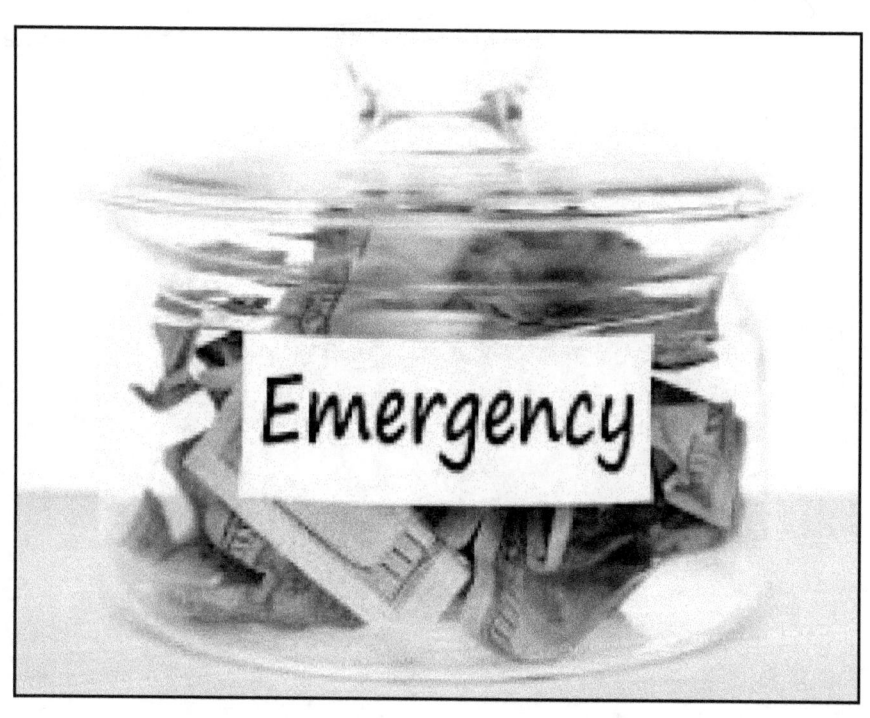

# 11. Setting Aside Cash Reserves

One of the biggest problems small businesses typically experience is chronic cash shortage. What comes in goes out almost immediately, and there's nothing left over! So, if something unexpected happens either personally or within the company that requires cash quickly, there's usually an insufficient amount of it on hand to take care of the problem. Also, there are other cash needs that a small business has that go unfunded for decades because all the cash is used up in the ongoing operation.

There are three main reasons why this happens:

1. Failure to identify and include cash reserves in the company's cash flow budget.

2. Failure to assign a high priority to the need for funding identified cash reserves.

3. A tendency for owners to become comfortable with their operating expense performance once all the bills are being regularly paid instead of constantly looking for ways to reduce operating expenses and improve efficiency.

A Reserve by definition is a particular cash account that has been separated out of normal operating cash and designated for a particular need in the future. The safe way to manage reserves is to set the reserved cash funds aside in a bank account fully separate from the account that handles normal operating cash. By doing that the reserved cash is not so easy to get to when an emergency arises and the owner might be tempted to dip into reserves instead of meeting the problem with ongoing cash generation.

The essence of the three reasons for never-funded reserve needs is that they're typically overlooked or procrastinated on by the small business owner. But the way it should work is that once a need for reserved funds is identified, it should be assigned a high enough priority so that the related funds will flow to it monthly from operating revenue instead of as an afterthought out of the rare occasions when cash is left over at the end of the period after all the other bills have been paid. Some people even pay some operating cost bills early instead of funding the reserves which at the least ought to be looked at on the same level of priority as the other bills.

Following now are four major kinds of Cash Reserves that should carry a high priority in your small business:

## Payroll Tax Fund

If you have employees, you'll be collecting payroll taxes from your employees on behalf of the state and federal governments. Those funds are no longer yours the moment you deduct them from your employees' paychecks. They belong to the taxing authority and you are now a trustee for those funds until you have turned them over to the government along with the required accounting and paperwork. Payroll Tax monies should ALWAYS be set aside into a separate bank account so they aren't comingled with your operating cash. Over the years I have seen a number of small business owners get confused and use payroll tax funds for operating cash needs so that the cash isn't available when it comes time to pay the state.

DO NO DO THIS! Be a good steward of the government's funds and in doing that you'll learn how to treat the other reserves that you set up. In other words, if the small business owner would faithfully move the cash over from the operating account into the other reserve accounts and then treat the reserve money as if it belongs to somebody else, then the chance of bringing the funds back into the operating side of the business will be minimized.

## Contingency Fund

One of the most typical signs of under-capitalization in small business is the inability to pay immediate cash for unexpected emergencies. When those things happen, and believe me they WILL happen, the company with no cash has to pay for it with additional, involuntary indebtedness. That debt will then have to be repaid in the future from revenue that's already committed to the ongoing operating needs of the company. The additional debt payments put a strain on the operation and make the cash shortage even greater. If you have enough unanticipated emergencies with no cash to pay for them, you'll eventually go out of business!

Many financial pundits recommend that small businesses need to work up to a Contingency Reserve of 3 to 6 months of average operating costs.[9] There are other factors involved in deriving the optimum amount for a particular business but this is a reasonable target for the typical scenario.

One thing to be clear about before moving on is that this Reserve Fund is for the contingency needs of the company, not for personal needs. The family also needs to have a contingency in their personal budget and we recommend an amount between $2,500 as an initial level up to about 6 months of gross income. Gross income is the amount of salary the owner receives from the small business BEFORE any deductions.

## Savings Fund

When you get into small business ownership and it has become your main source of income, you'll want to arrange to SAVE some of your profits. If you worked for somebody in the past then they might have provided some sort of matching savings plan as part of a benefits package where you were able to put some of your money into a savings plan and it was "matched" at some level by

---

[9] https://www.score.org/blog/how-much-cash-should-small-business-keep-reserve

your employer. Now that you're working for your own company, you'll need to try to reproduce that same kind of plan: you put a part of your salary into a savings account that your company provides and the company matches that with a similar contribution. You'll want to confer with a CPA and Estate Planner to be sure that you set this program up so that you enjoy the optimum effect on your overall tax situation.

Among other things you will need to become familiar with the guidelines for IRA deductions. IRA stands for *Individual Retirement Accounts* and taxpayers are allowed to deduct a portion of their taxable income and deposit it into a formal retirement savings account. The formulas for dealing with IRA's are beyond the scope of this publication and are subject to change. Also, there are two different kinds of IRA's, tax deferred and tax paid which will figure into your future retirement plans. So, you should consult with your CPA to determine how much you can deduct from your income to help stimulate your retirement savings as advantageously as possible.

One of the potential problems that small business owners get into is that they PROCRASTINATE on setting aside savings. In the beginning of the business venture, cash flow is tight and the business owner is focusing on getting all the current bills paid and on using available capital to expand the business. Before you know it, twenty years have passed by and still no savings plan. Now everything is going to cost more and the reality is, if you ever expect to retire to some less active level in the future after age 65, you'll not be able to come close to continuing your standard of living at a similar level that you've been enjoying unless you have savings that have been invested and have grown sufficiently to provide you with continuing income for life. The big questions that need to be asked and answered by the entrepreneur as early as possible are these:

1. What age do I want to assume as a retirement target? Most entrepreneurs retire later in life but at some point we all have to slow down.

2. How much income will I need at that time to continue living at the same or a higher standard of living? Most people assume they will spend less after retirement on living expenses but actually the opposite is more likely because of additional traveling expenses. And don't forget to include the expected negative effects on the value of the dollar caused by inflation.

3. Based on the amount of income I want to receive after retiring, how much of an estate do I need to accumulate by my retirement date?

4. How is that accumulated savings going to be distributed back to my family and me and what happens if I live a lot longer than the actuarial forecast?

5. How will my spouse and family be cared for if I should die younger than the actuarial forecast?

There are two kinds of professionals you'll need to consult with to develop intelligent answers to these questions: the first is your CPA and the second is your Insurance/Estate Planning professional. You'll need the CPA to be sure you set up the accounting correctly and you'll need the estate planner to help you answer these five key questions.

The basic idea is that your Savings Fund should consist of two parts: the conservative, low-risk part and the investment-growth part. The younger you are when you start your fund, the more aggressive you can be, reaching for higher rates of growth with higher risk investments. But there should always be the two parts and few people are that organized because they usually put all their savings into high risk growth funds when they're starting. Then when they get older they're still heavily invested in high risk funds until they retire and suddenly put everything into CD's that have the lowest return on investment there is other than putting all your savings under your mattress.

A healthy estate needs to be built up with the following major components:

- Cash
- Real Estate
- Securities Investments
- Life Insurance
- Safe Insurance Annuities you cannot outlive

- Disability Insurance
- Tax Protection including trusts, family ownership, etc.
- The value of your small business
- Etc. as recommended by your Estate Planner

The purpose of this publication is to simply point out that you need to consider these things and not procrastinate until you're almost ready to retire and you're trying to figure out something to make up for lost time. When you are first starting your business, develop a budget form that fits your operation and INCLUDE these Reserve Funds in the form even though at the beginning you may not have enough cash flow to fund them. Put them in the form anyway so you don't forget them and one day you WILL be able to fund those reserves with a high priority.

## Self-Funded Medical Insurance

If your company grows because of all your preparation and smart management, there may come a day when it would be in the cash flow interests of your company to consider self–funding your employee medical insurance. This isn't the appropriate publication to go into very much detail about this subject but it's something to make a mental note of for the future. You will need to have a fund set up for this purpose and you'll arrange with an appropriate administration company to handle the claims for your company. For many small businesses this will be a way to increase cash flow.

## Special Projects Fund

From time-to-time you will see a future need for your company to spend funds for a special project. It could be new equipment or an office expansion or any of a number of needs that are large enough that they can't be paid for in cash out of the current operation. Rather than move ahead with the project by going into debt, you could consider setting aside cash for the project each month until the necessary amount has been accumulated in Reserve and you can proceed with a cash purchase. The key to it is that once the need has been identified you are disciplined enough to continue setting aside the funds on a regular basis until the target amount has been accumulated. Not everything the small business needs has to necessarily generate related indebtedness and not everything has to be purchased immediately. Why not wait a while if you can to avoid the additional debt and the related strain on your cash flow.

In concluding this chapter, the main takeaway is that successful business requires discipline combined with administrative and financial knowledge. You don't have to know all the details but you DO need to know enough about these issues to call in professionals and experts in those fields that can provide you with good counsel that will make you and your company more successful.

FORCE your company to have enough cash on hand by using that discipline and by not procrastinating. Start early and keep it going!

# Why You Should Consider an HSA-Qualifying Insurance Policy during the Enrollment Period

One of the most underutilized tax strategies by small business owners is the use of a health savings account (HSA). Not only is it a flexible tool for helping to pay for current and future healthcare costs, but it can be a fantastic tax-savings strategy as well. Everyone should at least consider the HSA as an option when purchasing insurance during the enrollment period. Enrollment periods run from November 1 of the current year until January 31 of the following year.

Essentially, the HSA is much like an IRA that operates as a tax-favored savings account for healthcare. The only requirement to qualify for one is that you have a qualifying high-deductible health insurance plan.

Once you have the proper insurance, HSA contributions can be valid deductions on the front page of a taxpayer's Form 1040. Account balances grow tax-free, and distributions can be used immediately—and tax-free—for qualifying healthcare expenses. The way it works is that the high-deductible health insurance policy would cover major medical expenses above the amount of your deductibles and your deductibles are paid out of your HSA cash Reserve. It's a little complicated so discuss it with your professional team.

By the way, if you and your family are really healthy and don't use the saved HSA for healthcare, you can use the funds like a typical IRA after age 59 ½.

Also, to know what medical expenses qualify under an HSA, check out the long list in IRS Publication 502.

## Benefits of an HSA

Created by Congress in 2001, HSAs are perfect for individuals or families who consider themselves "generally healthy," and can afford the risks and costs of a high-deductible insurance policy. Here's a sampling of some of the benefits of HSAs:

### Save on Taxes

Not only are HSAs pre-tax accounts, but contributions to them are deductible from your gross pay amount. Since contributions can be deducted on the front page of your tax return, an HSA could potentially put you into a lower tax bracket.

### Spend the Money on Qualifying Expenses, Tax-Free

As long as you're using the money for health expenses—and odds are good that there will be more of them when you're older—your HSA could essentially act like a Roth IRA, in that Roth withdrawals made after retirement are not taxed.

## Save Money on Insurance Premiums and Healthcare Costs

HSA-qualifying health insurance policies generally carry lower premiums, which can save your business' hard-earned profits. Moreover, the ability to pay cash for healthcare costs allows you to negotiate for lower cost services. It might also motivate you to be healthier.

## It Can Help Pay for Your Retirement

After you turn 59 1/2, there's an option to make withdrawals for non-healthcare expenses, on which you'll pay federal income taxes. If you opt for this choice, the HSA then acts much like a traditional IRA, since the HSA holder pays ordinary income taxes on non-medical related withdrawals. There's also the added perk of not being bound by mandatory disbursements usually required by traditional IRAs.

## It Can Be an Investment Vehicle

HSAs allow you to invest the money in much the same way you invest an IRA. You can even invest HSA funds in real estate. So, in a sense, your healthcare savings could also help you buy a rental property.

It's generally advisable, however, to stick to more liquid investments if you have a health condition or are at risk of developing one. You want the money available in case of a medical emergency, which means you will also most likely want lower-risk investments.

## Is There Anything Else You Need to Know About HSAs?

Again, the only catch to qualify for the HSA and get a deduction in the current tax year is that you *have* a high-deductible health insurance policy (HDHP) in place before the enrollment period is over on January 31st.

Providing sufficient healthcare is not just about having a smart business sense. It can also be a smart tax choice. Before you make that decision, however, consult your team and review your financial statements to see if choosing an HSA-qualifying plan makes sense for your business.[10]

---

[10] Intuit Quick Books, Small Business Center, by Mark J. Kohler

*Thanks be to God who gives us the victory through our Lord Jesus Christ.*

1 Corinthians 15:57

*Thanks be to God who always leads us in triumph in Christ.*

2 Corinthians 2:14

*I can do all things through Him who strengthens me.*

Philippians 4:13

# 12. The Importance of Giving Your Business to God

The way I think about things, the most important advice I can give someone about being in business for oneself is that in order to have a successful venture, you should make Jesus your CEO. However, if you're not interested in a relationship with Him at this time, please feel free to skip this chapter because I would prefer not to pressure anyone. You can always come back to it later if you change your mind. God leaves it to each person to make his/her own decisions about the subject of relationship. Some folks want to have one and many don't and there are plenty of small business owners, in fact most of them, who don't pursue the relationship this chapter is talking about.

But if you DO want to know more, let's continue. In the long run you will not be able to have real success in things if you try to do everything yourself and take all the burdens home with you every night. And there WILL be burdens because all the challenges that come up will be yours instead of some big corporate employer like you used to work for. Indeed, being in business for yourself can be a blessing or a curse depending upon your mindset when you go into it.

When most people talk about being a success in business they're usually just talking about the financial part of it. The thought is you're a success if you make a lot of money. But finance is only part of it. You can be a big success financially and a bust emotionally. You can be making a lot of money and at the same time be under a huge amount of stress to the point of affecting your health. You can be financially well off but worried all the time about how you're going to keep it, or anxious about what would happen to you if you lost everything or afraid that some competitor is going to come around and take away everything you have.

But you can make Jesus your CEO and decide from the outset that you're not going to allow yourself to be subjected to all the pressure. And as you're approaching the end of this publication, if you don't know Jesus yet you can meet Him if you want to so you can start working together. The good news is that there's help waiting for anyone who will receive it by faith. All you have to do is ask for help, believe that you receive it and then speak out to others that you believe (Romans 10:9).

So, if you have never invited Jesus to become the Lord of your life, you can do so today by saying the following simple prayer:

*Jesus I believe in you and I believe that you were resurrected from the grave so that I can be born again and receive eternal life. Therefore, I receive you today as my Lord and Savior and I thank you for forgiving my sins.*

If you were sincere as you prayed this prayer, God has already come into your life and you are a new creation.

Congratulations! Now ask the Lord to lead you to a good bible teaching church where you can be developed to fulfill your potential in the Kingdom of God. And please send us an e-mail advising your decision so we can rejoice for you in our prayers. If you're unable to find a church, give us a call and we'll help you find a good one.

Now you are ready to make Jesus your CEO. When you have to make a decision, ask the Holy Spirit what you should do and then step out in Faith and do what you hear Him say. If you're presented with a problem or a burden don't carry it around yourself, give it to Jesus. You're not equipped to carry burdens around but He is and He wants to do all your heavy lifting for you.

And lastly, always seek first the Kingdom of God with your business. Put the Kingdom of God as your first priority ahead of your business and you won't go wrong. In fact, you can't go wrong. Do what you do for the Kingdom of God and success will follow you everywhere. It's all about the Kingdom and it's all about Jesus. Find out how to fit into that scenario and you will never regret going into business for yourself.

# 13. Summary of the Steps for Owning a Small Business

As we come to the end of this special book, I thought it would be helpful to summarize in one confined place all of the various points we've gone over so you can have a checklist for the future. Some of the points listed here have been reviewed in more detail than others but that's the nature of a book like this. The subject is broad and complex and a book that would cover everything would have to be several major telephone books thick.

No one can master this subject anyway just by reading a book. If that were possible, I think more people would be doing it. Anyway, you don't have to know everything before you get started but you ought to at least be familiar with the highlights and be aware that these things are out there to be learned in the future from further study and from experience, the latter of which is the best teacher, if the student survives.

If you can more or less follow the steps listed in this chapter and focus your attention on UNDERSTANDING how small business financial issues work, you will greatly increase your probability of success. Remember that historically 70 percent of all small businesses fail during their first five years of life; but if you have a modest understanding of what you've covered in this book, your chances of success will be 90 percent. Said another way: without knowledge seven out of ten new small business ventures FAIL. However, nine out of ten will SUCCEED if the entrepreneurs have a basic understanding of the principles presented in this book.

A. Following are the main *Preliminary Steps* to be accomplished before the startup of the new business:

   1. Set up a program that will result in eventual personal debt elimination. You don't have to be completely debt free before you start up but you need to have ALREADY designed and implemented a program.

   2. You need to have purchased a computer and know how to use its BASIC functionality.

   3. You need to know how to research on the Internet any business question that can come up.

   4. You need to have at least read this book from cover to cover and have a basic understanding of the financial parts.

   5. If you are a Christian believer, you need to dedicate your forthcoming small business to God.

B. The *Ten Key Steps to Starting a New Business* can be summarized as follows:

   1. Come up with a clever idea for your new business.

   2. Make an Internet study and find your own niche in your area of interest.

3. Come up with a clever name that articulates your new business and register it with your home state usually with the Secretary of State.

4. Open a bank account in the new name of your company. You can start out as a sole proprietorship and incorporate later.

5. Be sure you have progressed enough to be able to interpret the main financial statements discussed in this book. You also need to find an accountant who will be helping you with the financial aspects of your new business including the interpretations of your financial statements.

6. Make a basic Business Plan with a related cost analysis based on a forecast of how you expect your new business to perform. Yes, you will be ESTIMATING based on what you reasonably could expect to happen after your startup.

7. Make a Capitalization Plan which is a determination of how much money you will need to start up and how you will go about getting those funds accumulated.

8. Develop a low cost website. If you are low-tech limited like most small business entrepreneurs, you can use a template service like *Go Daddy Web Builder* and come out with a nice enough FREE website that will adequately meet your early needs.

9. Take a Quick Books instruction course and open your own Quick Books account. This is where you will record your sales and operating expenses and prepare your financial statements. You need to be able to enter your transactions YOURSELF.

10.	Make your first sale and record it YOURSELF on Quick Books.

C. Following are the main *Follow Up Steps* to be accomplished AFTER the startup of your new business:

1. Read continuously about business finance and never stop learning.

2. Monitor your competitors and keep track of what they are doing so you will know what adjustments need to be made.

3. Take a Social Media workshop and find out how to apply what you learn to increase your sales.

4. Complete your program to get out of all personal indebtedness.

5. Write a blog to become an expert in your field and then write a book about how you became successful.

Please refer to this Check List as often as you need to as you take the next steps toward your new start up and may the Lord fully bless your efforts. If you get into a bind about something, feel free to call us with a question or two. You may also want to consider our Mentoring Program with a low monthly cost, especially during the first months and years of your small business.

We want to see you succeed and let us hear from you as your personal testimony develops.

# 14. Some Final Thoughts

The purpose of this publication is to INTRODUCE you to a complicated subject. Therefore, the foregoing ideas should serve as a list of basic considerations to get you started thinking about all the various aspects of going into business for yourself. Talk to other people you respect and most importantly talk to people who have demonstrated entrepreneurial SUCCESS in their past so you can be advised from experience instead of opinion. Spend some time doing research to learn what it takes to be a successful entrepreneur. Buy some books on the subject and study to be informed. Avoid the temptation to step out impatiently, impetuously and unprepared.

At the beginning of this book we mentioned some negative considerations about being in business for oneself. This was not to discourage you from starting your own business but to encourage you to be fully informed before you take action. The fact is, we are hopeful that in due course an increasing number of people will want to move out of big corporations, where they have become dependent on a secular materialistic system, to oversee their own business. The chance for full success in business and in life is dramatically increased if you consult God as you go along, if you don't get in a hurry and if you prepare adequately for what you're about to do.

If you need help with questions that develop as you're preparing to go into business for yourself, please feel free to call us toll free at any time: (800) 357-4223. There is no charge just for talking things over: just mention that you have acquired this book and have some questions that weren't answered in it. We'll be happy to talk to you because no one can publish a complete publication on such a complicated subject. It's entirely predictable that you may come up with some issues that weren't anticipated.

## About Make A Way Ministries

For your information, *Make A Way Ministries, Inc.* is the publisher of this report and a 501 C-3 non-profit corporation. The Ministry is fully able to provide efficient service to consumers anywhere in the US. You can reach them as follows:

> Make A Way Ministries
> P.O. Box 1164
> Granbury, Texas 76048
>
> Local:      (817) 533-9499
> Local:      (305) 271-5094
> Toll Free:  (800) 357-4223
> Fax:        (305) 271-1826
>
> Email:      cfc@creditcounseling.net
> Web Site:   www.creditcounseling.net

*Make A Way Ministries* has been providing credit and financial counseling across the U.S. since 1987. All counseling is based on biblical principles and great care is taken to provide service that truly benefits our clients. We would never recommend a service to you just to take your money. On the contrary, we promise to recommend services only when they will be a benefit and a blessing. We pray that God will bless your efforts and reward you with His promised prosperity in accordance with His will for your life.

## Donations

If you would like to make a donation to help cover the cost of this publication, please make your offering payable to *Make A Way Ministries* and send it to the address shown above. By the Word of God we're certain that He will multiply your donation back to you. Gifts to *Make A Way Ministries* are normally tax deductible. May God bless you with His abundant harvest in return for sowing your precious seed into this Ministry!

# APPENDIX ONE:

# How to Apply for an SBA Loan

# Introduction

As you now know, most small businesses fail during their first five years of life. The tragic statistic is that 75% of them WILL fail based on past experience. The reason they will fail is that the owners don't possess enough business knowledge when they start their businesses and those businesses tend to be undercapitalized.

There's nothing that can replace business knowledge and get success instead of failure. No business knowledge = no success. That's the equation that almost ALWAYS confirms itself even though millions of people continue trying to prove it wrong.

Under capitalization is another matter. In fact, the federal government has set up an operation called the *Small Business Administration (SBA)* that specializes in making available training and capital to small business people to help them succeed instead of fail. If you conclude that your business can support some amount of indebtedness in order to have sufficient capitalization available, the SBA may be a good place to look.

The way it works is that the SBA guarantees loans through the banks of your choice assuming you meet all of the requirements. Some banks specialize in handling these kinds of loans and it's probably smart to look for one and they will usually have a Loan Officer on their team that is particularly knowledgeable.

In the remainder of this Appendix you will find a series of articles that will help you prepare for the pursuit of an SBA loan. Be prepared for a process with a lot of details but hopefully at the end you will find the optimum capitalization for your small business.

# Loan Application Checklist

Once you have decided to apply for a loan guaranteed by the SBA, you will need to collect the appropriate documents for your application. The SBA does not provide direct loans. The process starts with your local lender, working within SBA guidelines.

Use the checklist below to ensure you have everything the lender will ask for to complete your application. Once your loan package is complete, your lender will submit it to the SBA.

1. **SBA Loan Application** – To begin the process, you will need to complete an SBA loan application form at the following URL:

   • Borrower Information Form – SBA Form 1919
   https://www.sba.gov/sites/default/files/SBA%20Form%201919%204-28-14_review.pdf

2. **Personal Background and Financial Statement** – To assess your eligibility, the SBA also requires you to complete the following forms that can be accessed on-line at the indicated URL addresses:

   • *Statement of Personal History* - SBA Form 912

   https://www.sba.gov/sites/default/files/forms/SBA%20%20Form%20912%20%202-13.pdf

   • *Personal Financial Statement* - SBA Form 413

   https://www.sba.gov/sites/default/files/forms/SBA_Form_413_7a-504-SBG.pdf

3. **Business Financial Statements** – To support your application and demonstrate your ability to repay the loan, prepare and include the following financial statements:

   - *Profit and Loss (P&L) Statement* – This must be current within 180 days of your application. Also include supplementary schedules from the last three fiscal years.

   - *Projected Financial Statements* – Include a detailed, one-year projection of income and finances and attach a written explanation as to how you expect to achieve this projection.

4. **Ownership and Affiliations** – Include a list of names and addresses of any subsidiaries and affiliates, including concerns in which you hold a controlling interest and other concerns that may be affiliated by stock ownership, franchise, proposed merger or otherwise with you.

5. **Business Certificate/License** – Your original business license or certificate of doing business. If your business is a corporation, stamp your corporate seal on the SBA loan application form.

6. **Loan Application History** – Include records of any loans you may have applied for in the past.

7. **Income Tax Returns** – Include signed *personal* and *business* federal income tax returns of your business' principals for previous three years.

8. **Résumés** – Include personal résumés for each principal.

9.   **Business Overview and History** – Provide a brief history of the business and its challenges. Include an explanation of why the SBA loan is needed and how it will help the business.

10.   **Business Lease** – Include a copy of your business lease, or note from your landlord, giving terms of proposed lease.

11.   **If You are Purchasing an Existing Business** – The following information is needed for purchasing an existing business:

- Current balance sheet and P&L statement of business to be purchased
- Previous two years federal income tax returns of the business
- Proposed Bill of Sale including Terms of Sale
- Asking price with schedule of inventory, machinery and equipment, furniture and fixtures

# 5 Tips for Successfully Navigating the SBA Loan Application Process

By Caron Beesley, SBA Contributor
Published: February 19, 2013
Updated: September 3, 2015

In the market for a business loan? Heard about SBA loans but not really sure how they work or how to go about applying for one?

The following are common questions that small business owners have about SBA loan programs and the loan application process.

## 1. How do SBA loans work?

While the SBA does offer numerous loan programs to help small business owners finance their businesses, it doesn't actually lend businesses the money. Instead, a bank makes the loan, which is backed by the SBA. This allows the bank to take a little more risk than they otherwise might.

So this means that if you are seeking a business loan and don't qualify for a traditional bank loan, perhaps because you don't have the collateral or years in business to justify the loan, the government can help – although you still need to work primarily with a bank.

## 2. Who makes the decision that an SBA loan is right for my business?

If you've been turned down for a traditional bank loan, or are curious about SBA loan programs, where should you start? Should you go to the bank and ask for an SBA loan, or would they instinctively guide you towards one? While your local SBA district office can help explain the available loan programs and determine your eligibility for them, you'll need to find a local SBA lender to kick-start the application process. These banks and financial institutions can help you determine which loan program might be right for you, whether it's a traditional bank loan or an SBA-backed loan. They are also your point of contact for processing your loan application.

## 3. How do I determine which SBA loan is right for me?

The SBA offers numerous loan programs depending on your business profile, financing needs, growth plans and so on. There are a number of ways to identify the right loan program for your business.

If you are in the early stages of exploring your financing options, check out the SBA's Online Loans and Grants Search Tool. Answer a few quick questions about your business and the tool will suggest government financing programs for which you might qualify.

Once you've done your research, consult your local SBA District Office and ask them to steer you towards a few SBA lenders in your area so that you can be sure you're getting the right loan program for your business – and the right bank!

## 4. How should I prepare for my meeting with the bank?

Preparation is key and it's important to understand some of the criteria that might influence your eligibility for an

SBA loan. These include credit factors – such as making timely debt payments (payment on existing credit relationships, both business and personal, is considered an indicator of your ability to repay a loan), cash flow projections and your debt-to-worth ratio. Collateral and working capital are other factors that may impact eligibility.

SBA offers guidance on all the factors that lenders look at here.

You'll also need to ensure you are in good standing with your state treasury and the IRS (i.e., you've paid all taxes owed).

And don't forget the most important document – your business plan with at least three years of financial projections; a view of what you'll do with the proceeds of the loan; and solid proof that you know your industry and target market. This is particularly important for start-ups that don't have a financial history. The bank will base its decision on your industry experience and future plans.

If you don't have a business plan, check out SBA's Build your Business Plan Tool – a step-by-step guide to help you get started. You can save the plan as you go and download it when you're done.

**5. What do I need to complete my SBA loan application?**

An incomplete loan application won't do you any favors with the bank and could slow down the entire loan process. Familiarize yourself in advance with the key components of the loan application – from the right forms, to the necessary background information. Refer to this SBA Loan Application Checklist to ensure you have all your i's dotted and t's crossed. SBA also offers a free online training course: How to Prepare a Loan Package.

# Business Loans – What Lenders Look for and Tips for Winning Them Over

By <u>Caron Beesley</u>, SBA Contributor
Published: January 22, 2013
Updated: September 3, 2015

Securing small business financing can be challenging. Whether you are just starting out or looking to grow, banks and lending institutions can be rigorous in their lending review practices.

For example, businesses with few assets to their name may find it hard to secure a traditional loan. Other business owners may not be able to provide the reassurance that lenders seek to alleviate their concerns that your business may fail and the loan won't get repaid. So when you approach a lender, it's just as important to understand the basis on which loans are made as it is to stack up your financials and business plan.

So what are lenders looking for in a potential loan applicant? Here's what you need to know.

## Loan Applicants Need to Check off Several Boxes

What are loan officers looking for when approached about a loan? Here are some basic "must-haves" that the ideal candidate might be expected to evidence:

- That you have sufficient assets, financial reserves and personal collateral to endure business fluctuations (and still pay off your loan).

- As an existing business owner, you'll need to show that you have solid cash flow, sufficient to repay the loan.

- New businesses need to evidence that they have a track record of profitability and success in a similar business endeavor.

Let's face it, that's a tricky list for any prospective or existing small business! So what are your options? Proving your creditworthiness is still possible, with some planning and preparation.

**How to Prove Your Creditworthiness**

Bankers need to make money, and while they may have an ideal candidate in mind, even they have to compromise—this is where your opportunity lies. The trick is to demonstrate, using other means, that you are a creditworthy business owner. For example, if you are new to this business, can you show success in managing a similar business another field (even if you weren't the owner)? Perhaps you've owned or managed a profitable business in a different industry? Lending officers might be more agreeable to your application if you can show that you supplement your own experience with that of someone who also has success in the field.

Putting yourself in the lender's shoes is a good starting point. It's much like a job interview, where you form an understanding of the type of candidate the employer is looking for and prepare your application and anticipate questions accordingly. Ask yourself: "Why should this lender think my business can succeed where others have failed?" and have a thorough answer prepared, plus a detailed explanation of how the money will be used and your plan for paying it off.

**Step Back and Prepare**

Key to this preparation is a solid business plan, good personal and business credit, and some expert help. The following SBA resources and tools can help guide you down this preparation path:

- **Build a Business Plan Online Tool** – Putting pen to paper to write a business plan isn't the easiest of tasks. Check out this new tool from SBA that guides small business owners through the process of creating a basic, downloadable business plan—and offers pointers on essential elements like cash flow and financial projections. The great thing about this tool is you can build a plan in smaller bites, save your progress and return at your leisure.

- **Clean Up Your Credit** – Business credit is an asset and considered an economic resource that makes up the financial foundation of a company. Lenders look for assets. SBA guest blogger Marco Carbajo blogs regularly about how to build your business and personal credit to help secure financing. Check out his article: *How To Build Business Credit For Your Start Up*, and view more of Marco's articles here on the SBA website.

- **Consult an Expert** – Whether you need help finding the right loan for your business or a guiding hand that can help you through the application process, don't feel that you have to go it alone. Local Small Business Development Centers, Women's Business

Centers, and SCORE (a mentoring organization for small businesses) can help you through the process. Find one of these groups in your community.

## Can't Get a Business Loan? Consider Alternative Financing from SBA Loan Programs

If you or your lender decides that you aren't the right candidate for a traditional business loan, you still have options. Consider an SBA Loan Program. The SBA doesn't lend businesses money; instead, these programs take the risk away from the banks and encourage them to make loans to small business owners by guaranteeing part of the loan.

Check out these additional online learning resources that can help you navigate the SBA loan process:

# APPENDIX TWO:

# Eight Basic Secrets of Financial Success

The following article was written a number of years ago and talks about the eight major things in life that produce financial success. Everyone who starts a business needs to be mindful of these principles and if you are, it's way more likely that you will turn out to be a financial success.

# EIGHT BASIC SECRETS OF FINANCIAL SUCCESS
## (AKA: HOW TO HANDLE YOUR MONEY)

Almost everybody wants to be a financial success. Even the ones who believe they'll never be successful would like to be if they could just find a way. The problem is most people don't know the way; they don't know how to do it. They think it's about making more money. But most rich people didn't get to be rich because somebody paid them more money or because one day they finally won the lottery. No, they became rich because they had a plan to go somewhere, they pursued that plan day after day and they did a good job of HANDLING whatever money they had on hand along the way. And oh by the way, most so-called rich people are NOT financially successful either.

What does it mean then to be *financially successful?* If you were living in some third-world country you'd be *financially successful* if you had enough to eat, if you had fresh water to drink and if you had a roof over your head. But since you live in the USA where materialism is king, the standards for financial success are higher. We want to have a lot of possessions and our definition of success is reserved for people who have a lot of them including big houses, big cars, a lot of expensive clothes, etc. But did you know MOST of the people who go around showing off those kinds of things either owe some creditor for them or they acquired a lot of it illegally? They're usually tortured by fear that they could lose all their acquired stuff and that they could be left with nothing, stripped of all their assets and standing in Bankruptcy Court.

Friend, financial success is NOT about how much money and possessions you control. It's NOT about how much money you make. No, it's about the quality of your life that has resulted from how you've HANDLED the money that's come your way over the last 7 to 10 years of your life. And the measure of your success is how you feel about what you have: are you at peace with it all or do you live in fear, losing sleep or running from your creditors all the time? Is your credit rating so negative you're afraid to go and interview for a better job because you think no one will hire you? Are you embarrassed for someone to look at your credit reports?

A person who's *financially successful* is content, lives comfortably within his/her level of income, has all their essential needs met, has enough contingency funds set aside to deal with the emergencies of life, and has money left over to sow into the Kingdom of God and to bless family and other folks when those occasions arise. A person who's *financially successful* is someone who makes wise decisions with the long-range future in mind instead of just for the moment. A person who's *financial successful* is someone who lives by faith and trusts that God will take care of them. A person who's *financially successful* is not trying to get rich but the blessing of prosperity always finds them out anyway without having to strive for it.

In 1987 we started a credit counseling ministry here in Miami and over the years we've come in contact with tens of thousands of folks. As you'd expect almost all of them had some kind of credit problem. They came to us because they needed help in getting themselves out of some money situation that was holding them in bondage. So for a number of years now we've had a unique opportunity to come to some conclusions about what it takes to be *financially successful* and based on that experience we've been able to summarize the various qualities that produce SUCCESS down to eight of the basic PRACTICAL requirements that will ALWAYS produce good results. If you'll do these eight things it's virtually GUARANTEED that you WILL be a financial success in 7 years or less.

## 1. You Must Have a Family Budget and Live By It

Most people don't have a budget. In fact, more than 85% of folks in the US have NEVER had a personal or family budget, wouldn't know how to put one together if they tried and think they don't need one. Nothing could be further from the truth. No operating entity from families to corporations that has money coming in and going out should try to make it all work without a budget. Lack of planning is one of the main reasons people are financially unsuccessful because they have no idea where the money they make is going.

Accompanying this article is a simple one-page Family Budget form that you can use to get organized. How do you spend your money? If you spend more than you bring in you'll either have to go broke or use indebtedness to make up the difference. *Financial success* comes from spending LESS than what you make, not more. And the way to be sure you'll always spend less is to write down ahead of time how you're going to spend your money. And then keep track of how you actually spent it compared to your plan. Most families live paycheck to paycheck and are essentially insolvent. Insolvency is when you owe more than you're worth. But in our experience we've only encountered a very few families who were budgeting before they came to see us because families who budget usually don't have financial problems. An essential requirement for *financial success* is to live by a budget. Nothing will work until you're willing to make this step.

A budget should be used as a guide to making your expenditures. It doesn't have to be some legal thing but at the end of the month you want to come out with totally expenditures that are less than your income. How you get to that objective every month is not as important as getting there. If during the month you see that you're going to overrun one of your budget categories then reassign the funds from one of the other budget categories where you can spend less than the budget. If you can come out at the end of the month CONSISTENTLY with your expenses less than your income you will be *financially successful* in no time.

## 2. You Must Avoid Indebtedness

We live in a society where almost everyone is in debt. It's part of our way of life and we don't think too much about it. If we want something we just take out a credit card or open a new charge account and more often than not we have only a vague idea of how we're going to pay back a new debt. The whole financial system in this country is based on the assumption that the consumer is willing to go into debt and pay their creditors outrageous amounts of interest for letting them borrow their money. And since consumers are willing to do it the banks and other creditors are eager to attract people who have relatively decent credit ratings and are willing to go into debt.

But here's a key point to know if you want to be *financially successful*: you can NEVER be *financial successful* and in debt at the same time. Indebtedness is the most formidable obstacle to success there is. It MUST be eliminated and then avoided like the plague because it's so toxic to success. Virtually 100% of all consumers who can be considered *financially successful* are DEBT FREE. The absolute <u>wrong</u> way to handle money is to go into debt to purchase possessions you think you can't wait for. To change that picture and have even a chance to be successful, you'll have to make a final no-compromise decision to stop using debt and then take action to make it happen to become DEBT FREE. No exceptions!

### 3. You Must ALWAYS Pay ALL Your Bills on Time

A lot of people are kind of blasé about paying their bills on time. They don't pay any attention to the official payment dates and just pay their bills when they get around to it. Other folks are trying to make their payments as late as possible just before the creditor cuts them off thinking they're winning some kind of dumb game. It's dumb because the system GREATLY favors the people who make all their payments on time and gives them the reputation as people of good character.

But did you know that every late payment you make is reported by your creditors as DEROGATORY information to the three national credit bureaus? And did you know that a pattern of late payments causes your FICO Scores to be significantly reduced? Lower scores means you pay higher interest. Lower scores mean you won't be seriously considered for the best jobs because employers interpret a history of late payments as an indication of a flawed character and irresponsibility. Lower scores mean your insurance costs will be higher. And most companies charge late fees which greatly increase the real cost of your credit.

So the correct way to handle your money is to be on top of your payments and pay them even before the due dates so you can be sure to not ever be late. Make it one of your highest priorities as it should be. Plan your payments for the times during the month when you receive your income and you know that you'll have the funds on hand. And don't forget that if you're mailing them you need to allow plenty of time for your checks to arrive at your creditors' offices. If they don't arrive on time they WILL be counted as late and you WILL have to pay late fees and you WILL be reported to the credit bureaus as having paid late. This is really, really important!

## 4. You Must Monitor Your Credit Reports

Most people have never seen their credit reports but if you have a social security number you definitely DO have credit reports. There're three national credit bureaus and each of them publishes a credit report that summarizes a lot of private information about every consumer in the country. Anyone that's specifically authorized by the law may review that private information about you by paying the appropriate fees to the credit bureaus. The publishing of private information is allowed by the law but credit bureaus are restricted as to how they may distribute the reports. Legally authorized users include prospective creditors, landlords, lenders, banks, insurance companies, prospective employers, etc.

Did you know that studies show that more than 70% of all credit reports contain errors or outdated information? Those errors could be costing you real money if they go on undetected because if they cause your FICO Scores to decrease, then your interest rates could go up. How're those errors detected? They'll be detected ONLY by concerned consumers who're regularly monitoring their credit reports. No one else will be looking for them. That means YOU have to be in charge of your own credit reports and insure that they are reflecting an accurate and as favorable picture of you as possible.

Another thing to be concerned about is that Identity Theft is the fastest growing white collar crime in the country. Most people find out about that they've been a victim of IT when they receive a bill or a call from a bill collector about a debt they never heard of before. But someone who is on top of their credit reports and is monitoring them every few months will catch a problem early in the process. Also, the smart consumer is probably going to have an alert service set up with the credit bureaus so the identity thieves will be unable to penetrate your defenses. The person who handles their money correctly is a person who PROTECTS their credit ratings and constantly monitors their credit reports.

You can obtain a FREE credit report annually from each of the three credit bureaus at:

www.annualcreditreport.com

We recommend down loading one at a time every four months during the year so that you're always working with recent information. You can also purchase one of the on-line monitoring services for about $15.00 per month. There're a number of good services and we particularly recommend the ones sold by the credit bureaus at the following web sites:

www.equifax.com
www.experian.com
www.transunion.com

5.  You Must Stay Away From Get Rich Quick Schemes

There were three main reasons why so many families have had financial problems because of the recession: 1) reduced income, 2) indebtedness and 3) using debt to invest in real estate thinking they were going to get rich in a few months. Certainly reduced income has been hard to deal with. Unemployment and cutbacks are still at difficult levels. But the people who have had the most trouble are the ones who were in a significant amount of debt BEFORE the recession. Folks who didn't have any debt at all have been able to weather the storm much more effectively. But the ones who're the worse off are the people who were going into sub-prime mortgage debt they shouldn't have been able to qualify for trying to "flip" real estate and get rich QUICK.

Very few rich people ever got there QUICKLY. It almost NEVER happens that way. A basic principle of handling money is that the QUICKER something is the more RISKY it is. Leading up to every recession or depression or what they used to call "panics" in the history of our economy there has ALWAYS been a large group of people who were trying to pursue some scheme to get rick QUICK. They are SPECULATORS who push up prices to artificial levels only to eventually see the bursting of those price bubbles where they lose all their money.

The moral of the story is stay out of get rich QUICK schemes and speculations. Avoid them like the plague! They may sound good but if it's QUICK it's going to be RISKY and the person who's pursuing a course to *financial success* should be trying to avoid RISK as much as possible. Becoming *financially successful* is a slow, purposeful, step-by-step process of following a good plan of living within your budget, staying out of debt, putting money aside in conservative, low-risk investments that won't disappear when the next recession comes along and being content to wait to buy things until you have accumulated enough CASH.

6. You Must Avoid Co-signing

Now this next one is going to be hard because eventually some friend or family member with a bad credit rating is going to come to you with your good credit rating and ask you to CO-SIGN with them to help them go into debt. Most people these days give in to those requests because they want to be loved by their families and they want to love them back by helping them "progress" in life. But, you MUST resist the temptation if you want to be *financially successful.*

When you CO-SIGN with someone for a debt you are telling the creditor that if your loved one defaults on that debt YOU will pay it off on their behalf. You are GUARANTEEING that the debt will be paid. Do you have the money set aside for that possibility; otherwise if your loved one defaults you have just gone into debt. If the financial system found it too risky to give credit to your loved one, why would you want to take on the creditor's responsibility by taking the risk on your own shoulders? We have seem time after time the good financial ratings of otherwise debt free people ruined by having CO-SIGNED a debt they were not able to pay for when their loved one defaulted.

You will just have to resist the temptation to GUARANTEE someone's debt. Why would you want to help someone go into debt when your value for yourself is to stay out of debt? No, tough love is better for both sides in these situations. The better approach would be to gift your money to your loved one as you can afford it into a savings account <u>that you control</u> with both parties contributing into that account as you've agreed together until there's enough money accumulated there to pay CASH for the thing they had originally wanted you to CO-SIGN for. Debt is NEVER the right answer for someone who's working to be *financially successful* and the hard truth is that CO-SIGNING often leads to debt!

## 7. You Must Have a Contingency Fund

The purpose of a Contingency Fund is to have money set aside to be used ONLY in the case of emergencies. We're all going to experience emergencies from time to time that we had no way to plan for. For example, you need a new battery for your car (they cost more than $100 these days) or new tires or your washer or dryer goes out or there's a medical emergency you hadn't planned for or whatever thing that could come up that you need to pay immediately. Most families have to go into debt to pay for those kinds of unexpected expenditures which means they incur related interest costs and their budgets are strained because of the additional monthly payment until the debt is paid off.

But the smart way to operate is to set aside provision for those unexpected occasions. We recommend that the minimum a family should have set aside is $2,000 and that it should be deposited into some special savings account that's not so easy for you to get access to and take out funds for expenditures that aren't really emergencies. Just start setting aside an affordable portion of each pay check with the objective of building up to the $2,000 recommended MINIMUM. With this amount you'll be fairly well covered for most emergencies.

But don't stop there. You want to go on and continue slowly building your Contingency Fund until it reaches 6 times your monthly gross earnings. If your gross salary/income (before payroll deductions) is for example $3,000 per month then you'll want your eventual Contingency Fund to reach an ultimate objective of $18,000. Why? So you'll be covered for a period of time if you lose your job or your hours are cut back or if another recession comes along or you have a medical issue that makes it impossible for you to work for a few months. If you have your 6-month fund put together and you minimize your living expenses while you're going through the storm, it will be relatively for you and won't have to go into debt to make it through. You'll come out on the other side still Debt Free and still *financially successful.*

## 8. You Must Study to Become Informed

Finally, if you want to be *financially successful* it's absolutely essential that you study and become informed about the financial industry and how it operates. Most people don't know anything about it and yet our money is one of our most important interests in life. Your quality of life depends largely on how you handle your money yet most people don't know anything about it. They don't think they have to know, they don't want to invest the time it takes to learn about it and so they stay financially ignorant and live life mostly in chronic lack and insufficiency... There is a scripture in the Bible that really fits this situation: *"people are destroyed for a lack of knowledge."* If you attach the importance to your financial situation that it deserves you WILL study and make it a regular part of your life.

There're books and magazines you should be reading, there're FREE workshops and seminars you could be attending, there're many, many financial newsletters you can subscribe to. And of course the financial information available on the Internet is inexhaustible. The only question is this: is financial success important enough to you that you'll put in the time and attention that's needed to qualify for it? People who're financially uninformed will NEVER be *financially successful* because they'll make too many costly mistakes. You cannot short cut what it takes to be successful. No, you have to methodically and faithfully and repeatedly and continually do ALL the little things that it takes to get to where you want to be. Frankly, handling money correctly should be one of your highest priorities in life even ahead of your own job because if you work hard to be good in your job and make a good salary only to waste away the money you make after you bring it home, what good did it do? You had in your hands the means to become *financially successful* but wasted the opportunity by failing to give it a high enough priority. So go study now and learn everything you can find on the subject of your finances. You'll NEVER regret it.

## Conclusions

As we wrap up this discussion, there're a few final key thoughts for you to always remember about becoming *financially successful:*

1) These eight basic secrets WILL produce financial success. It's guaranteed!
2) No matter the income level every person can be successful.
3) The only limits on your financial accomplishments are put there by you.
4) There're no short cuts to success.
5) You cannot circumvent the basic secrets we've discussed in this article.

If we can help you in any way please feel free to contact our ministry and when you call mention this article. Many of our services are FREE and our mission is to teach people what they need to know to be *financially successful.* Just call us at 305-271-5094 or toll free 1-800-357-4223. May God fully bless you and your family as you apply yourselves to the task of becoming *financial successful.*

# ABOUT THE AUTHOR

Dr. Bill Miller is an ordained cross-denominational minister, elder and the founder of a national nonprofit Christian organization called *Make A Way Ministries.* He has been involved in financial counseling and teaching since 1985 and has assisted tens of thousands of families to overcome financial problems and get on to financial success and victory.

He also pastored the bilingual (English/Spanish) *Faith Life Fellowship Church* in Miami Florida from 2007 until 2012.

Dr. Miller has published a bible-based financial e-newsletter called *Prosperous Life Newsletter* since January 1998 and has written more than 25 books about various financial topics with the purpose of helping families overcome financial problems on a practical level.

Make A Way Ministries started officially in 1987 by counseling Christian business people in Dade County, Florida. That form of counseling has always been a particular calling for this ministry and provided a wealth of experience to draw from for this book.

Dr. Bill was born in Houston, Texas a long time ago and is a graduate of *Texas Tech University* in Lubbock. He also holds a Doctorate in Ministry from *Miami Christian University.*

He currently lives happily and works busily with his wife Sherri in the historic community of Granbury, Texas.